DATE DUE

MAY 2 5 2011		
JUL 3 0 2011		

To my family

FAMILY OUTING

FAMILY OUTING

What Happened When I Found Out My Mother Was Gay

a memoir

TROY JOHNSON

Arcade Publishing • New York

FIRST EDITION

Frontispiece by Mike Elliott / iStockphoto

Some names and identifying characteristics have been changed.

Library of Congress Cataloging-in-Publication Data

Johnson, Troy, 1973–
  Family outing : what happened when I found out my mother was gay / Troy Johnson. —1st ed.
     p. cm.
  ISBN 978-1-55970-871-5 (alk. paper)
  1. Children of gay parents—United States—Biography. 2. Lesbian mothers—United States—Biography. 3. Family—United States. 4. Gender identity—United States. I. Title.
  HQ777.8.J64 2008
  306.874092—dc22
  [B]   2008006947

Published in the United States by Arcade Publishing, Inc., New York
Distributed by Hachette Book Group USA

Visit our Web site at www.arcadepub.com

10 9 8 7 6 5 4 3 2 1

Designed by API

EB

PRINTED IN THE UNITED STATES OF AMERICA

I understand the importance of bondage
between a mother and child.

—Dan Quayle

CONTENTS

Author's Note

Before I Offend You . . .

SEX MAKES US. OR IT MAIMS US. Either way, we remember our first awkward, sloppy kiss. We remember that maiden pubic hair, bursting through like a tiny flag for the empire of adulthood. We vividly recall both minutes of losing our virginity.

I'm an adult, heterosexual male. Easy enough. Now all I need is a fertile woman, a dopey-looking dog, and an irrationally large vehicle in order to achieve eternal happiness. But life is never that simple.

I grew up with a gay parent when Reagan was president, before the era of "Don't ask, don't tell." Then it was, "Where the homos at? Let's smoke 'em out and string 'em up!"

When I was first trying to understand my situation, I turned to books for information and advice. All I found was feel-good psychobabble about "embracing our differences" and "disarming our bigotries."

Blah, blah, blah, I thought. *Of course.* But what was it really like for kids like me? Someone needed to tell it real.

My life wasn't turning out like *Chicken Soup for the Souls of Children with Homosexual Parents*. It was more like the movie *KIDS* and the book *Thirteen*. Someone needed to say exactly what a shallow, self-absorbed teenager thought about the situation while he was experiencing it — in a way that people who may not be interested in the issue could gawk, chuckle, learn, and relate.

So that's what I've done. In the process, I've revealed skeletons I thought I wouldn't even tell priests. On my death bed. At gunpoint.

But as I was writing this book, it became more than about having a gay parent. It became a riff on the madness of sex, the delusions of suburban delinquency, the comedy of worthlessness, and the salvation of getting a clue. It became my life.

Gays have families now. They're no longer just single people with strange roommates and expensive furniture. Their right to marry and raise children has become a presidential hot-button issue. Listening to politicians and religious leaders pontificating on the issue prompted me to tell my story — the story of a kid who lived it.

I have not held back anything, including how having a gay parent creates new problems for the American family. If it sets the gay rights movement back a few years, so be it. If it helps Ellen Degeneres become president, that's also cool. If it has no impact whatsoever because only you and two gay bloggers in Minnesota are reading it, that's fine, too. It's more important that *Family Outing* be honest.

Family Outing takes on the convoluted Western idea of sexual identity. Consider it a report from the sidelines of the turf war between heteros and homos, politicians and peers, celebrities and grandmas. I like to think the story is universal — all people sooner or later have to decide if they're straight, gay, bisexual, asexual, or just want to hump footwear.

But I also realize my story is unique. Very few people have forced themselves to imagine having sex with the same gender just to see if it would make them vomit. Even fewer have attempted to take LSD for the first time in a psychiatric ward. I hope.

It is also crass — not for shock value but because that's how life is when you're a teenage boy. It wasn't "Behold the nice homosexual woman." It was "Hey, get a load of the clam bumper!" Vulgarity defines adolescence more than Tipper Gore would like it to.

Despite what you may think as you read this, I am on good terms with my mother. Great terms, actually. I tell her I love her not because it's a Pavlovian reflex. I get choked up every time she gives me a lesbian-strength bear hug to say good-bye.

She is, and always will be, the woman in my life.

FAMILY OUTING

Chapter

1

Tattle Dyke and Freckle Spawn

THERE ARE CERTAIN SECRETS YOU CAN TELL only the people you care about. They start small — *I like science-fiction movies* — and grow successively more incriminating as the relationship progresses. *I wet the bed until I was seven.* Eventually, you reach the moment when you're sure the person with bad teeth and an unpredictable hairline is part of your destiny. Only then do you drop the big ones.

I once stole a child's Halloween candy.

The smell of armpit funk gets me hard.

I am your mother, and I have gay sex less than twenty feet from where you sleep.

Mom never had the chance to tell me that last one. The previous two were mine. As a series of expensive therapy sessions would later reveal, she had intended to tell me and my sister that she was gay.

But it's a slippery slope — a gateway revelation. If she

told us that, she'd also have to tell us that we'd be socially outcast by our peers until they had their first "experimental phase" in college. Or when they realized that being a bigot, like admitting you've seen every Steven Seagal movie, drastically reduces your chances of getting laid.

The day I learned Mom was gay started out boringly enough. I was ten years old, and it was a cold morning for San Diego. Dressed in a brown woman-suit, my mother cracked open the door of my bedroom. She looked like one of Charlie's Angels who'd spent some quality time at the buffet line. Her black hair was bowl-cut, and she had thick glasses that screamed *I'm blind, really blind!*

She was a physical therapist in charge of the spinal cord division at the Veterans Hospital. She spent her days trying to convince people who had risked their lives for their country to do rehabilitation exercises that they didn't want to do.

"Troy. *Troooyyyyyy*," she called. "Time to get up."

I was running late. I was always running late. It was a pattern that would later lose me girlfriends and good jobs.

"Troy, you little shit, we're going to miss the bus!" my sister yelled a half hour later.

"I KNOW! I'm FINE!"

My sister unwillingly took on the role of surrogate parent at an early age. She was absolutely shit at the job, and I was even worse as a surrogate child. There were two reasons Kim had to play mom. First, my mother had an acute fear of not being able to support the family, so she was a workaholic. Second, she wasn't ready to "break the news" to my sister and me. So if she and her girlfriend wanted to hold hands or kiss or make those immensely disturbing cooing sounds that lovers make, she knew they'd have to do it somewhere else.

So my sister made sure I brushed my teeth, made the school bus on time, and didn't spend hours trying to catch bits of boobs between the blocked reception of the *Playboy* channel.

Ten minutes later I still wasn't ready.

"Troy! I'm *leaving*! If you miss the bus, Mom is going to kill you!"

"Whatever!" I screamed. "Just go! You're not my mother!"

The front door slammed shut. Seven minutes to figure out which shirt in my laundry basket smelled least like rotten fruit and to slap a couple pieces of bologna on bread.

School days were always like this. Every day, my sister yelled at me for lagging. Every day she left and acted as though Mom would beat me with a cooking spoon if I missed school. And every day, I ran up just as the last kid was getting onto the Poway Unified School District bus. Sure, I'd have to sit next to the girl with head lice, but at least I didn't have to wait at the bus stop with the other kids, one of whom would eventually call me "Monkey Ears" and flick them with his finger.

But this morning the doorbell rang. The doorbell *never* rang before school. I froze and tried to hold my breath, hoping whoever rang it would go away.

It rang again.

I hadn't yet been arrested. So I had no reason to suspect the mysterious doorbell ringer wore a uniform.

There were only two possibilities. The first was our neighbor, Mr. Crasnick. He was an evil old man who confiscated our kick balls whenever they flew into his yard. We explained that our errant cherry ball was proof that he lived among gifted athletes who would one day have sports drinks named after them.

"Mr. Crasnick, that's a *home run!*" we'd scream.

Mr. Crasnick didn't share in our excitement. One of the neighborhood mothers politely asked once that he refrain from confiscating the balls. Instead, she suggested, he might approach her and solve the situation amiably. I didn't hear his response, but I believe he told her to go fuck herself.

The other possibility was the church people. They'd come to our door and give us free comic books with drawings of smiling children hanging out with Jesus and assorted farm animals. For years I thought heaven was a petting zoo.

When I peered out of the peephole, it was worse than the Nazi neighbor or the Jesus freaks. It was my mother's best friend, whom we'll call Tattle Dyke. She stood there with her eldest daughter, whom we'll call Freckle Spawn.

Oh my God, Mom's dead.

Dark, but that's what I thought.

Tattle Dyke was unnaturally gaunt, her metabolism souped up like a stock car from a lifetime of smoking. She had slivers for lips, as if they'd been surgically tucked and pinned to her gums. Her helmet of black hair looked like a compressed afro, and her facial expression was always that of a person who had just watched a relative die.

I despised Tattle Dyke. My mother liked her, I concluded, because she made strawberry shortcake from scratch. They had been close since I could remember, and for the last seven years we'd spent the majority of our lives together. It was excruciating.

Tattle Dyke treated my sister and me like houseflies — nuisances that were difficult to kill. If we asked her a question, she would sit literally for ten seconds before even acknowledging she heard us. So when I asked, "Tattle Dyke, can I have a Coke?" she pondered the sugar content, divided that number by the minutes until our bedtime, considered the questionable marketing tactics of the Coca-Cola corporation, and weighed all possible outcomes before replying, "No."

My mother once told us that her methodical communication came from her Cherokee heritage. Native Americans apparently preferred to ponder every question deeply rather than give an immediate, superficial response. It made me empathize with early Europeans who had shot them.

I had a choice — hide and miss school, or open the door and rush past Tattle Dyke and her daughter. I figured the latter should work fine enough. I grabbed my bag lunch — bologna sandwich, two Twinkies, twelve Red Vines — slung my latchkey around my neck, and opened the door.

"Hey Tattle Dyke! My mom's already left for work. I'm gonna miss my bus, so I gotta jam!" I said.

"We know," Tattle Dyke said, stone-faced. "Do you mind if we come in and talk to you?"

Freckle Spawn stared at her shoes.

"I would, but I'm gonna miss my bus," I reiterated, before using my sister's false threat to my advantage. "My mom will beat me with a spoon."

"Troy, this is important — it's *about* your mom. I think you'll be excused from school today."

She's definitely dead.

I wanted to cry. Skipping school with adult permission ranked high on my list of cool activities, but my gut told me Tattle Dyke wasn't about to whip out a six-pack of soda and three tickets to Disneyland.

I stepped aside and let them in. I prayed to Jesus the Petting Zoo Zookeeper that some Vietnam vet hadn't screamed "Die, you fuckin' Charlie!" as he sprayed the room with bullets.

"I have to get something out of the dryer," I told them. Another lie. I went to the dryer and pretended to fondle an article of clothing. They followed.

"Damn, not ready yet," I said of my imaginary sweater. They were standing there. I was trapped.

"Troy, come sit with me," Tattle Dyke said, sitting cross-legged on the floor.

This proved she at least knew something about me. Even if a perfectly good sofa was available, I always sat on the floor. I often slept in the linen closet because I was afraid of the dark and liked to be in small spaces where I could feel in control.

So I sat. Freckle Spawn didn't look at me. Her sullen eyes scanned the room, as if watching an imaginary friend she had invented because her mom was lame.

The pregnant pause between us entered its fifth trimester before Tattle Dyke finally said it.

"Troy," she said, "your mom is a homosexual." Her face was serious and grave. It was a look that might also accompany statements like "The Chargers just moved to Los Angeles" or "Space Ghost has three weeks to live."

I just sat there, too confused to run or cry.

Honestly, I didn't know what a "homosexual" was. It sounded like something that Rick Marshall would say to his son Will on *Land of the Lost* when they discovered a particularly nasty species of dinosaur that ate humans.

"Your mother and I are — well, *were* — lovers. Just like normal moms and dads, except we're both women. Do you know what a lesbian is?"

"Yes," I said. Now I was crying.

Again, I was lying. I had heard the word, possibly even used it. But I had no idea what it meant. I had a gut feeling, however, that it had something to do with the fact that Tattle Dyke and my mother had been sleeping in the same room for years.

At this point, my most vivid sexual encounter involved Richard Pryor. My father had accidentally taken me to see a film called *Stir Crazy* starring Pryor and Gene Wilder. It was R-rated and included a nude scene in a strip bar. When the dancer's four-foot boobs flopped onto the giant screen, I remember being embarrassed. I wasn't supposed to see them — it was an adult thing. I looked over at my father, my eyes wild with excitement and confusion. He stared straight ahead and refused to meet my gaze. He was probably thinking he was the worst father in the world because, two years prior, I had discovered his *Playboy* collection in his closet. Naturally, I invited all of my friends over to check it out.

Eventually, my best friend A.J. told his mother that we were spending every afternoon gawking at airbrushed areolas. The next day, A.J.'s mother gave my dad an earful about how he was a good man, but should be ashamed for leaving his nudie stack where her impressionable boy could find it and get an erection before he knew what to do with it. My father still recounts this as one of the most embarrassing days of his life. I disagree — it was definitely the white-man afro-perm he sported at his second wedding.

If I had actually *read* the nudie magazines, I would have learned that "lesbians" were beautiful women who worked at construction sites and liked to have group sex with other employees during their lunch breaks. But we just looked at the pictures, and those sorts of photos don't say a thousand words to a child. They say: "You have no idea what you're looking at, do you?"

My parents never talked to me about sex, which, in retrospect, is odd. They're both highly educated, communicative people. Maybe they just hoped that when I finally got an erection, I wouldn't stick it in something with a live electrical current. *Sexuality* was still a word I'd overheard in adults' jokes, or caught briefly while flipping the channel past PBS to get to *The Dukes of Hazzard*. And now, before bothering to provide a definition of the root word, Tattle Dyke had tossed on a prefix — and it was apparent that "homo" wasn't a positive addition.

Tattle Dyke outing my mother was my first sex talk. Normal kids got the birds and the bees. Mine would more appropriately have been called "the symbiotic relationship between ornithological species and *Psithyrus vestalis*."

Tattle Dyke made lesbians sound like people who went to the doctor every day until their hair fell out. The look in Freckle Spawn's eyes gave me the feeling that it made her, my sister, and me "alternative" kids — the flawed people. I'd have to spend my allowance on black eye makeup and start cutting myself for fun.

This especially sucked because I harbored a deep, intense craving to be normal. Now all my efforts would be wasted. I could become prom king later in life, and I'd be standing onstage with my perfect teeth and my stylish haircut and not a spec of lint on my tuxedo. "God, he's got everything — the girl, the bone structure, fame," a less amazing teenager would say as he watched my coronation.

"Yeah," his date would whisper, "but his mother's a lesbian."

"No shit?!"

"Nope. Total scissor sister."

"Oh. Poor guy."

Everyone would instantly pity me. They would clap louder, like they do for kids with crossed eyes and puffy faces who win Olympic medals for running the 100-yard dash in under an hour. A roar of sympathetic hoots and hollers would rise from the crowd as the DJ dropped the needle down on Gloria Gaynor's "I Will Survive."

If my mother had told me herself that she was gay, I could have seen the love in her eyes. She would have cried — my mother could cry if the donut shop ran out of apple fritters. She cried because she thought she might cry.

"I'm a lesbian, Troy. It means that I love women in the same way that Dad and I used to love each other," she might have said. "Some people think it's strange, or even wrong, but it's not. It's something from the bottom of my heart that I can't ignore anymore."

It was the way I felt for Heather Locklear on *T.J. Hooker.*

My mother would have explained to me how some people hated her for her lesbianism — but they were the same people who thought they were poor because the Jews had hidden all the money. I, the kid with the monkey ears, would be able to relate.

We would have hugged. I would have bought her a flannel shirt.

Instead, Tattle Dyke told me. A woman I'd like to have removed from this world if possible. Not dead, mind you, just *removed* somehow — maybe traded to another planet for testing purposes. Even worse, I'd be stuck with her for hours before my father could come to my rescue.

The only thing my father detests more than confrontation is rap music. He's a tragically kind man — the sort of person who would give you his shoes if you told him they were nice. As divorced fathers go, he was great. He asked for extra custody days and canceled dates with pretty, vacuous women if we wanted to roller-skate or torture starfish at Sea World.

Tattle Dyke continued explaining until he arrived.

But I didn't trust her, so I tuned her out and listened to my body sob.

Dad arrived to find his own personal hell. His son sat on the floor, a sniveling wreck. A lesbian with the personality of a paperweight had just outed his ex-wife, and the paperweight's daughter was sitting in his favorite leather chair — a chair, I should add, that he gave up in the divorce and that our black lab had used as a scratching post ever since.

My father comforted me. I laid my head in his lap, and he stroked my hair. Our family expressed love like dog owners.

That day was a blur of verbal reinforcements like "Oh buddy" and "Your mom loves you so much. This doesn't change that." Dad called Mom at work to tell her what was going on. I imagined her snapping the leg of a crippled marine in her rage, driving over to Tattle Dyke's house to suffocate her cairn terrier with a plastic bag, then coming home to deal with this.

At some point I couldn't cry anymore and was bored with feeling sorry for myself. Dad and Tattle Dyke took me for my very first submarine sandwich that day — white bread, gobs of mayonnaise, fatty meats, and Italian dressing.

I loved that sandwich. It was tasty, and I could be seen in public with it and no one would whisper.

Chapter

2

To Deal or Not to Deal

ONE OF MY FAVORITE MOVIES IS *Anchorman*, a comedy starring Will Ferrell and featuring the foibles of a local 1970s TV news team. In a pivotal scene, the male anchors storm into the news director's office, having just learned the station has hired a female reporter.

"Don't get me wrong, I *loooove* the ladies," says the offbeat entertainment reporter with a cologne fetish. "I mean, they rev my engines. But they don't belong in the newsroom!"

"It's anchorMAN, not anchorLADY!" adds the sports anchor with a shovel-shaped forehead.

Finally, the mildly retarded weatherman slams his hands on the news director's desk and screams. "I DON'T KNOW WHAT WE'RE YELLING ABOUT!!!" Then he skulks off camera.

I played the role of the mildly retarded weatherman during my mother's outing. I expressed anger, calling her a liar and accusing her of making our family weird. But I may as well have been screaming at her for failing to properly evaluate her variable annuity. I didn't really know what we were yelling about.

Whatever it was, everyone seemed to think it was the ax leaning against our family tree.

I formed a collage of the reactions around me. Tattle Dyke treated homosexuality like a terminal illness. My sister acted as if Mom had hidden a long-lost sibling in a closet and had finally just made soap of the child. My father tarnished his perfect work attendance to deal with this tragedy. I was allowed to stay home from school, as if some relative we didn't think was a total douche bag had died.

It seemed like at any time cops would bust through the door and say, "Ms. Roy? You're under arrest for lesbianism. You have the right to remain silent . . ." I'd have to visit Cellblock L in order to get a bear hug or bore her to death with the pitch-by-pitch account of my baseball game.

My mother sat at the dining room table — crushed. She was a sobbing, snorting, snot-nozzle who vaguely resembled a human being. Between apologies and pleas, she explained that she'd been talking to a shrink. They had devised — carefully, constructively — a head-shrunk way to introduce this information to our half-developed brains.

They probably would have explained the birds and the bees. Then, how sometimes the bees hung out with bees and the birds with birds. This bird-on-bird action, while uncommon, wasn't something that displeased Mother Nature. Ronald Reagan and the pope, yes, but not Mother Nature.

The sight of her crying activated, as it always did, my stab-the-person-who-made-her-cry reflex. My mother and I were soul mates. Our love for each other was intense, molecular. Early on, I sensed she needed as much protection as I did. Every inch of me wanted to sit in her lap and pet her head. She'd done that for me when I cut my own hair the day before school photos and it looked as if an epileptic had groomed me. She petted my head every time my sky fell.

She held out her arms. Hugs cured everything in our house. But for the first time in my life, I turned my back on her and went to my room.

The next day, the whole family went to the shrink to pick through the wreckage. The shrink was a good-natured stereotype: a Jewish man with too much beard and too many college degrees. He surfed and had a sandbox dotted with little army men. Failing his "has this child been properly socialized" test, no doubt, I started pretending they were blowing each other's plastic guts out.

"OK . . . well, wow," he started. "Kim, Troy, Cathie, Rich — seems like we've got a situation, don't we?"

Kim rolled her eyes and crossed her arms. If she had telekinetic powers, twelve bloody knives would have flown across the room into the wall.

"Well, first, I need to tell you, Kim and Troy, that your mother and I had been discussing how to tell you about her situation. She *did* plan on telling you. Unfortunately, she didn't get the chance."

"She had years of chances," Kim snapped. "At least Tattle Dyke was honest with us."

Mom burst into tears. Kim said more things to assist in that endeavor. Dad petted Kim's head. I shot a plastic AK-47 into the face of my tiny plastic enemy.

After a while, the shrink noticed my silence and said, "Troy, you haven't said anything. How do you feel about all this?"

Absorbed in Operation Polymer Death War, I simply shrugged. "It's her life. She should be able to do whatever she wants. She's not hurting anyone," I said.

A better shrink would have seen the passive aggression in my response — which, if allowed to persist, would ferment into a deep-seated maelstrom that would manifest itself in a lengthy police record. Not this guy.

He laughed. "Well, Troy, we'll let you know when we're all as mature as you are." Then he turned the focus back on my sister.

I said what I said because I wanted to believe it. I loved my mom — that deep, atomic love. Who cared if she was gay? Why was that so bad? She didn't send me to the store for milk so that she and her friends could stick needles in their arms until they saw Jesus. But, of course, I cared. I was angry, confused, insecure, and selfish.

Partially because I saw myself as my mother's protector

and partially because this drama was *way* out of my fucking league, I wasted hundreds of dollars of my parents' money pretending to be the most mature person in therapy.

During these sessions, my sister kicked and screamed and attacked, getting it all out. This probably explains why she was able to raise three fantastic, well-mannered children before I landed a stable job.

All my trauma would surface later on.

Chapter

3

The Secret of
the Locked Door

TWO YEARS BEFORE TATTLE DYKE dropped the big news, we had left San Diego. My mother enrolled at the University of Southern California to get her master's in physical therapy. We moved to a nearby city called Downey, a magical place just outside Los Angeles. In Downey, standard police procedure for a traffic ticket is to ask for the driver's license and registration only *after* the barrel of a gun is firmly pressed against the driver's temple.

I remember the first day I saw this. My mother and I were driving back from the grocery store when we passed a car pulled over by the police. This alone was fascinating, because in the late '70s cops were cool and had their own TV show called *CHiPs*, starring a hunky Latino cop named Poncharello. He was always trying to get his stiff, white partner to disco with girls in bikinis just seconds after a major drug bust.

I didn't realize until we were parallel that the police officer had aimed his gun directly at the driver's head. Strangely, the twenty-something black man being held at gunpoint seemed perfectly calm. He sat there wearing a mild look of disdain, as though the cop had just told him a bad joke.

"Mom! He's aiming his gun right at that man's *head*!" I yelled, tossing my own head out the window. "Drive around the block! I wanna get a closer look!"

"Troy *Michael*, sit down!" she barked, grabbing my pants leg. I was standing on my seat with half of my body out the window, staring back so as not to miss any flying brain parts. I imagine that's the moment my mother realized what a mighty cauldron of hell she'd brought her kids to.

A friend of mine had his bike stolen in Downey. My own bike had been stolen when I was in third grade. The difference here was that my friend's bike was stolen while he was still riding it.

Apparently the nice group of twelve-year-old boys with half-shirts and smoker's voices had forgotten theirs — or maybe had them confiscated in a police raid. So they stopped my friend and told him to get off. A little voice of conscience could remedy the situation, though, surely. Usually, if you reminded people that you'd be telling their moms, they came to their senses and you all shared a soda.

"Hey!" I yelled. "Leave him alone. That's not your bike!"

The big kid with bad acne and a black Yosemite Sam

T-shirt turned to me with the trained, steely eyes of an adolescent bike snatcher. "You want yours stolen, too?" he snarled.

"No," I sulked.

"Then *shut up.*"

The only thing worse than your friend having his bike stolen is having yours stolen. Again.

Downey kids lived by a code: If you didn't get what you wanted for Christmas, you took it from the smallest person on the block. If no small person was readily available, you loitered near the grocery store loading dock, smoking a cigarette and hocking loogies until one arrived.

Other than the stolen bike, white cops pointing guns at black drivers who didn't use turn signals, and the fourteen-year-old girl next door who said, "Let's see that little thing" while she tried to unbutton my pants — Downey seemed like a pretty safe place.

Before we moved, my mother made my sister run for student government at her school. She said it built character — like we were dramaturges or something.

Given my sister's God-given talent to create detailed pencil spreadsheets of every household rule I broke (handed to our mother with the suggestion, "As your consultant, I advise you to get rid of him"), she ran for student body secretary and lost.

Later my mother made me run. My dad explained that "the VP really runs the show." The VP could order bombs dropped on countries with unpronounceable names, but he was rarely depicted in cartoons as having abnormally large facial features. Plus, I had a reasonable, British sense of ambition. If there was a big cheese in any situation, I preferred to be the medium cheese. If porn stars were the loftiest profession in American society, I would have aimed for fluffer.

A stringent campaign of stickers that read, "A vote for Troy Johnson is a vote for candy," led me to victory. As part of my campaign promise fulfillment, I sold Jell-O Pudding Pops at lunchtime as a fund-raiser for the school. The treasurer and I sold one for every four we embezzled. They were delicious.

By the end of my term, I had developed such a contemptible sense of self-importance that the other kids started flattening my bike tires. But I didn't care. I could have their colored pencils revoked or simply have them eliminated. I was enjoying my first true taste of being an egomaniacal prick, which I later discovered led to company cars and secretaries with nice tits.

When I tell friends I spent two years in Downey, they look at me as though I know how to bribe prison guards for smokes and porn. One friend informed me that Downey was well documented in travel magazines as the place where they break white people into little pieces and "use 'em as a base for soup."

At the end of fourth grade, my mother graduated from USC magna cum laude, ranked among the top six physical therapy grads in the nation. She's what adults who ruin parties call a smart cookie. We packed up all of our stuff — except the floating thing that apparently was once a goldfish — and moved back to San Diego.

We moved to a temporary apartment while we waited

patiently for the tenants, as my sister put it, "to get the fuck out of our house" in Rancho Peñasquitos. While my sister and I were thrilled to be back in San Diego, what she found in our mother's bedroom tempered her excitement.

I was gone the day she found it, and wouldn't learn about the discovery until years later. But Tattle Dyke's daughters were there — the one with the eating disorder and the one who looked as if she had an eating disorder. We were one big, rarely happy family by that time. While my sister had been hoping for one less brother and I for one less sister, these two additional siblings snuck into the picture. They possessed natural abilities to piss us off, so they fit right in.

My sister went into my mother's room to look for something — cash, no doubt — and found something else altogether.

"Gay Rodeo!" the magazine clipping announced in a large, exciting font. You could almost hear the self-conscious *yeehaws*.

My poor mother. Cutting out a magazine article about a fun social outing that you want to attend with your lover ranks high on the list of "Cute Things Done By People Who Are Screwing." She probably thought they'd go out to a steak dinner, dressed up in matching checkered shirts, and spend a romantic night amid the smell of barbecue sauce and cow dung.

Kim made the mistake of thinking that she and Tattle Dyke's daughters could analyze the evidence together.

"Do you think our mothers are lesbians?" she asked, passing the clipping to them.

Freckle Spawn, the older one, shared her insight on the matter: "Your mom might be, but ours isn't."

As if our mothers went into the bedroom and Tattle Dyke just read a book while my mother flapped her arms in an elaborate lesbian dance that converts straight women or makes it rain. It's understandable, though. We kids of gay parents are blessed with denial, a superpower that's been helping alcoholics order one another around for centuries.

I had known since I was seven that there was something different about Mom's and Tattle Dyke's relationship — but it was just a *feeling*. I didn't have the vocabulary to actually define it. *Lesbian* — like *paternity suit* and *autoerotic asphyxiation* — wasn't a term that adults talked about with their kids in the early '80s. All I knew was that she and Tattle Dyke both entered a bedroom at night and locked the door. If we knocked on that door, it took them quite a bit of time to open up. They also seemed out of breath, as though they might be exercising. At midnight.

I tried to understand this through my own experiences. But my friends and I only went behind locked doors if we wanted to set things on fire or trade sniffs of our sisters' underwear. Mom didn't seem like an underwear sniffer.

I could have walked into a room where my mother was surrounded by a half-dozen women in various states of undress, but I still would have refused to put two and two together. Even if each of these six women swore my mother had paid big money for this and showed me the credit card receipt, I would have concluded that they were accomplished liars who worked at Citibank. I would then grab my mother by the hand and abscond into the night. I would help her land a leading-lady role in a movie starring Burt Reynolds, the straightest man in Hollywood. He drove a Camaro and had a moustache. My mother's entire role would consist of kissing him, with no speaking parts whatsoever.

Such is the power of denial. Because when you finally accept that, *Shit, Mom really is gay*, life gets a lot harder real quick.

Chapter

4

Mommy's Little Lesbian

MY MOTHER CLAIMS SHE WASN'T TRYING to turn my sister and me into little gay people. I believe her, but there were times I had my doubts.

Gloria Steinem gave my mom her parenting philosophy. Steinem went over to India in the late '50s, and instead of returning with weed and a sitar like the Beatles, she came back with bad hair and a conscience. She founded *Ms.* magazine and wrote an article that exposed the degrading work conditions of *Playboy* bunnies. Thanks to her, men in the 1970s masturbated with a heavy heart.

Steinem also suggested, "We need to raise boys like girls."

Bitch.

Because of this Steinem woman, my sister and I never knew which public bathroom to enter. Because of her, we rarely received gender-specific toys or clothes.

We also grew up on Marlo Thomas's *Free to Be . . . You and Me*, a children's record featuring Alan Alda, Mel Brooks, Harry Belafonte, and other celebrities intent on ruining the lives of children. It similarly encouraged our parents to raise us as he-shes.

Following this philosophy, Mom signed Kim up for a soccer league. It was quite a show. There were no girls' leagues back then, so Kim had to play on a team with all boys. Required by the governing laws of youth soccer to give every member playing time, the coach occasionally said, "Johnson, you're in." My sister took one step over the line, where she folded her arms against her chest, turned her back to the playing field and didn't move. An inch. At all. The whole season.

The next year my mother signed my sister up for a girls' softball league. Every Saturday they returned home with veiled smiles and shrugs that suggested Kim had played rather poorly.

Actually, "poorly" suggests that she tried. For the two seasons that my mother forced her to play softball, Kim set the league record for live balls not reacted to, nor addressed in any way, as if the fielder might be uninterested, blind, or dead.

If she had to stand in front of other humans wearing a baseball cap and cleats, Kim was going to do it in a way that proved she wasn't a tomboy. Before games, she brushed and blow-dried her hair. She wore her cap so that it appeared to have been lightly tossed on her head, possibly by a cute, flirty boy.

She participated a bit more in softball than she had in soccer. She stood taller than most girls her age, so her teammates revered her from the start and assumed she had great physical abilities. They weren't entirely off base, either. She had proven the ability to balance herself on the backseat of my father's van, arch her back, and kick me square in the face. Girl had skills.

But the coach soon demoted Kim to right field, which is where coaches put girls who either suffer from muscular disorders or were forced into the sport by their feminist mothers. She put her hands in her pockets and daintily swayed from side to side, waving to friends or scanning the grass for four-leafed clovers.

If, God forbid, a ball was hit in her vicinity, she used her glove to protect her face and remained motionless until she heard it safely hit the ground nearby. Then she ran over, picked it up, and lobbed it in the direction of the apoplectic tomboy, yelling, "Hit your cutoff man!"

At the plate, Kim proved even less active. She could have exacted her revenge against my mother by taking lazy swings or walking toward first base when she hit the ball, but that apparently was too close to actually playing, so she simply didn't swing. Not once. At all. The whole season.

My mother had been a world-class junior tennis player and excelled in an adult softball league, so she couldn't relate to her daughter's lack of killer instinct on the field. After watching yet another motionless plate appearance, Mom had an idea and called my father.

"Look, Rich, we've got to do something about Kim's poor softball showing. I've got an idea. Why don't we give her a dollar for every swing she takes?"

Realizing his children responded better to money

than moral support, my father agreed. He didn't require Kim to line a double into the gap or that she even make contact. She simply had to take what appeared to be a half-hearted swing at the ball.

Kim didn't make a single dollar that year.

"If I hit the ball," she pleaded to my father, "some other girl might beat me out for the bench position."

Sure enough, she won the bench position hands down due to lack of competition. The coach put her into active duty only if her team was behind by 27 runs or if a mononucleosis epidemic broke out and he couldn't field the necessary positions.

Kim agreed to play catch with me exactly once. She and my mother had returned from yet another impressively sub-par performance. Kim flopped down on the couch, relieved to be home.

"Your brother's quite a pitcher," my mother said. "Troy, why don't you take your sister out in the yard and help her out a bit?"

Playing catch with girls is like playing Ping-Pong with a quadruple amputee, but I would do anything to get my sister to stop locking me in small, dark places. This was my chance to win her over by imparting essential wisdom about baseball.

I started with soft throws, but it wasn't five minutes before I hurled a ball at her that would have given her a reverse Adam's apple.

"Hey! I'm not going to play with you if you throw like a jerk!" she screamed. "I'm a *girl*!"

Not for long, I thought. This was my chance to dispose

of her. And because it happened during an innocent game of catch and not by, say, burning her at a stake, I would be exonerated. The judge would explain, "Although her death is a tragedy, we cannot blame the defendant for having such a great heater."

The next ball I threw caused Kim to shriek — which proved she'd never make it on a team of softball butches who could hit for average and block the plate.

But she was in no danger. The ball sailed far over her head and into the backyard of our neighbors. My sister threw down her mitt and stormed inside without saying a word. She used silence like a fist. The unspoken threat that later she might make me bleed was far more effective than calling me a "booger eater" during the heat of the moment.

Having failed to deform her, I climbed the fence and dropped into the Cracknells' backyard to find the ball.

Mr. Cracknell was my barber. He was also my savior. I was born with man-sized ears that protruded from my head like moose antlers on a midget. To save me from severe ridicule or having the best part of my lunch stolen by a normal-looking child, Mr. Cracknell let my hair grow over my ears so they had their own curtains. Of course, this just made them more conspicuous. My haircut pretty much screamed, *Holy goddamn! Look at the honkers on this kid! Genetics gone wrong! Three bucks for a full show!*

The sad part is that I honestly believed it looked okay. I valued Mr. Cracknell's skills.

My sister, on the other hand, loathed the woman who cut her hair.

"I look like a *boy*!" she screamed after every cut.

"Don't be silly," my mother always replied. "You look beautiful. It's a classic look."

If "classic" means that something conceals gender, then my sister's haircut was the epitome of classic. She really did look like a boy. I occasionally made matters worse by parading in front of her with a salad bowl on my head.

For my father's second wedding, his fiancée, Cindy, curled Kim's hair. Kim beamed with pride. In the photos, you can see a newfound sense of cuteness in her eyes. Instead of staring glassily at the camera like an emotionless sociopath with a bowl cut, she twinkled. Her smile was feminine and mischievous. She loved herself.

Her pride fell later, when she returned home. Mom looked at my sister as though she'd badmouthed Gloria Steinem in public. Kim burst into tears.

I assigned my sister's gender based on my mood. It would depend on, say, whether she had just let me snag a Snickers bar from her stash of Halloween candy. She kept her candy for months, rationing it, while I ate my entire haul in a couple of nights, then ran around like a mental patient in a burning building before collapsing into a diabetic coma. If she had shared, I would say, "No, Kim, you look pretty. You're so girly that this just makes it so that you're not *too girly.*"

But if she had just given me a facial contusion with the business end of a telephone, I'd say, "Well, at least I can tell people I got beat up by a boy!"

It all came to a head one night when my father took us out for dinner. An unwitting waiter approached our table. He took my father's order, then mine. Finally, he turned to my sister and asked, "And what would you like tonight, young man?"

Kim's boyish head dropped to her chest and began to weep uncontrollably. Normally this would have been cause for great joy on my part, but even I couldn't muster a victory snicker. The waiter had no idea what he'd done to her psyche. That this stranger thought my sister peed standing up had ruined her, and this was what complete ruin looked like.

She'll have the cyanide, medium rare.

Skirts for Kim were the exception rather than the rule. In Mom's ideal world, she would have built a steel cage around Kim's crotch and equipped it with sensors that detected boys' hands. If activated, a light borrowed from the set of *Batman* would project an image into the cloudy sky. Instead of a bat, though, it would be a vagina — and it would appear to be in distress.

My sister had exactly one skirt. It was a flower-print hand-me-down that spun out when she twirled. You could always spot my sister from a great distance when she wore that skirt. She was the one who was constantly spinning, the fringes of the skirt billowing around her. That and the dress she wore to my uncle's first wedding represented the only two girly pieces of clothing that she owned. The rest of her wardrobe was painfully unisex. I could borrow whatever I needed if my own clothes smelled like feet.

Nor was Kim allowed to pierce her ears or wear makeup, which literally drove her to crime. One day at the checkout line of a toy store, a tube of lip gloss fell from her pocket and clattered onto the floor. My mother just saw it as stealing. She didn't notice the subtext: desperate young girl resorts to stealing her idea of femininity from aisle 4.

But nothing so acutely highlighted my sister's plight as the toy store. Toy stores are partitioned like gymnasiums. There's a part for boys, and a part for girls. The boys' section is filled with guns, army men, sports equipment, and trucks. Lots and lots of trucks. These toys help boys grow up to be aggressors.

In the girls' section, every single surface is pink. If a toy arrives that isn't pink, an employee will take it out back and spray-paint it pink. There are beauty items, fake cooking appliances, and dolls. Lots and lots of dolls. If there is a stray piece of sporting equipment in this section, you may deduce that a little boy came over and pelted his sister with it while she was looking at dolls. These toys — when combined, at a legal age, with a man's penis — help girls grow up to be sperm receptacles.

My sister could have done without the E-Z Bake Oven. She had no interest in the vanity mirror dipped in glitter. All she wanted was a Barbie.

Barbie was not welcome in our household.

Barbie is the feminist movement's own personal Satan. After years of complaints from women's groups, Mattel eventually redesigned the doll so that her hips had a little extra cushion for pushin'. But in the 1970s, Barbie should have come with a Bulimic Accessory Kit — plastic laxatives, eroding teeth, and a sparkly butterfly clip to hold her hair back while she gave her all to the Thin-Maker Potty Seat.

Every one of my sister's friends had a Barbie, but my

mother would have rather allowed my sister to dance top-
less for a school talent show than buy her that doll. Kim
had to tell the other girls, "Well, no, I don't have one. But I
have this board game that increases your memory power!"
Mortifying.

Later, when Mom's sexuality sent the family spinning
into group therapy sessions, Kim brandished this little fact
as the ultimate proof of psychological abuse. "I never had a
Barbie!" she cried, wailing the words with such conviction
that Barbie might have been a metaphor for food, shelter,
love, and the American Dream.

Throughout our childhood, my sister secretly kept a
box underneath her bed. It was cardboard with flowers on
it. Inside was one imitation Barbie doll. Toy stores had the
Sunsational Malibu Barbie and Pink 'n' Pretty Barbie. My
sister had what she called White Trash Barbie. It was pa-
thetic, and it was her most valued possession on this earth.

My sister had drawn a picture and taped it to the outside of her box — a girl with short hair and a speech bubble
that read, "I'm a girl, not a boy!"

Whenever I was really angry with my sister, I con-
soled myself by destroying her stuff. She could beat me to
a pulp, so I attacked her inanimate objects. But never in a
million years would I touch that crappy little flower box.
My sister would let Mom take away her feminine identity,
but she would have defended that White Trash Barbie with
her life.

When Kim hit puberty, lipstick became an issue. We
lived in Downey at the time, and she befriended a girl
named Crystal who couldn't decide what she loved more:

heavy metal or hairspray. Crystal was a fascinatingly gro-
tesque child, the product of severe cutbacks at the Child
Protection Agency. She wore T-shirts she bought at con-
certs by bands like Iron Maiden and W.A.S.P. One shirt —
a replica of Iron Maiden's 1981 album *Killers* — featured
the image of a grinning zombie whose facial skin had rot-
ted away. The zombie held an ax dripping with blood
freshly liberated from the person begging for his life at the
creature's feet. Her W.A.S.P. T-shirt was less gruesome: a
close-up of a woman's panties, from which extended a ro-
tary saw blade below the words, "I Fuck Like A Beast."

In other words, you may have wanted to borrow this
twelve-year-old girl's records, but you certainly didn't want
to agitate her. Crystal's mental stability was like the game
Jenga, right before all the blocks tumble and people laugh
and cheer and die.

It was Crystal's makeup that no doubt attracted Kim
like a moth to a raging inferno. Crystal had eyeliner in a
wild assortment of colors — such as charcoal and black.
After years of prohibition, my sister wasn't satisfied with a
subtle shade of blue, so the two of them spent hours making each other look like dead people.

The first time I saw my sister in goth makeup, I knew
she had finally done something wrong. It was time to tattle.

"What the heck is all over your eyes?" I asked.

"None of your damn business," she replied.

"You look scary," I said.

"Twerp," she said. This meant the conversation was
over. It was her Jedi mistress way. As the years progressed,
her vocabulary took on the words *shitface* and *dickwad*, but

whenever she answered a question with a one-word insult, it meant one thing: she was through with you.

I thought about yelling after her that I was going to tattle, but I wasn't lying when I said she looked scary. If she didn't kill me in my sleep, I was quite sure Crystal would. Eventually the two of them stopped hanging out, either because of the natural fickleness of preteen friendships or because Crystal knocked over a liquor store and went on the lam.

In junior high, my sister began fighting for the right to put holes in her face. She had begged my mother for years to let her pierce her ears. Unsuccessful, she finally threatened to get them done at the mall. My mother was horrified. She imagined Kim being mutilated by a high school girl whose only qualification for the job was that she could wear a name tag. Defeated, my mother took Kim to the pediatrician's office and had her ears pierced by a doctor — who no doubt had had her own ears pierced at the mall.

My mother still maintains that these rules had nothing to do with being a lesbian. "It was all part of being a feminist," she said. "All of my feminist friends were doing the same stuff to make sure their daughters weren't sold on this fake sense of what a woman should be."

The problem is this: if a straight mother embraces feminist ideals, she's forward thinking. If a gay mother embraces feminism, she's a dyke with an agenda.

Anything *Cosmopolitan* recommended to my sister to make her look like the other girls, Mom translated into "like the other sluts." She was trying to protect Kim against becoming some man's toy, one who could cook and screw and fetch cold beers during critical moments of a football game. She was protecting her from the oppression of penis.

And my sister hated her for it.

My sister is now happily married with three children of her own — two boys and a daughter named Laura. Laura makes Barbie look like a bull dyke. My sister pierced Laura's ears when she was six months old. (We can only assume the doctor refused to do it when he cut the umbilical cord.) Laura owns approximately 4,723 dresses and four gallons of glitter-based makeup. I have it on good authority that she learned to apply lip gloss before she learned how to pee in a toilet. She is everything my sister wanted to be.

Kim bore the brunt of the unisex torture because my mother had a better understanding of what it meant to be objectified as a woman.

But Kim wasn't the only one.

Chapter

5

Mommy's Little Metrosexual

MY MOTHER TRIED TO RAISE ME as a compassionate human being. She didn't want me to grow into a man who giddily inhaled popcorn while watching news stories about genocide, or one who thought his role in fatherhood ended shortly after orgasm. She wanted me to cook, cry, and share.

And so, one year I got a doll for Christmas. I remember it vividly because a piece of me died that day. It was the piece that helps men belch at the dinner table and win at poker.

It was still dark outside when I emerged from my room. My mother had already plugged in the lights of our Christmas tree, which my sister and I had decorated. Kim very carefully strung ornaments so that they were equally, tastefully distributed. I, on the other hand, drowned the otherwise healthy-looking conifer in silver tinsel. It looked like a white trash tribute to Liberace.

The presents under the tree appeared to have been wrapped by stroke victims. Other women in my family treated gift-wrapping like an ancient art. They spent Christmas mornings oohing and ahhing over symmetrical flaps and perfectly folded corners. My mother found no joy in wrapping, so she handled it like the fishmonger at the supermarket. She'd slap a gift into a wad of the nearest available paper and cinch it off with Scotch tape. She wrapped like a man.

I was tearing through gifts when I came across something with blue eyes and long eyelashes. It wasn't an action figure like the Incredible Hulk or Shaun Cassidy from *The Hardy Boys*. It was the sort of flesh-colored infant that looks just human enough to be incredibly creepy. It came with a bottle that you were supposed to stick into its mouth and say comforting things like, "There you go, baby. That's right, baby. Hungry baby."

"Uh-oh," I said. "I think I got one of Kimmer's gifts." I showed the doll to my mother and my sister. Kim's eyes grew wide with excitement — not because the doll was that great but because it increased her overall gift count.

"No, that's yours, Troy," my mom said. "Dolls aren't just for girls."

"Oh," I replied, jumping up and down on my knees to fake a sense of joy. "Thanks!"

Some genetic mutation in my DNA made me physically unable to tell my mother I didn't like her gifts. My sister could delicately unfold the wrapping, look at a new wristwatch, and say, "Good try, Mom, but no. Did you keep the receipt?" I could open a box to see a T-shirt that said

"I'm a huge nerd! Ask me about it!" or unwrap, say, a doll, and I'd smile and tell my mother I loved it.

I named the doll Georgie after my favorite cartoon character, Curious George. (We had similar ears.) No one in the world — not even Midnight, our black lab — ever saw me coddling it or inserting the bottle into its mouth and saying "Oh, hungry baby. It's okay, Daddy's here." But a bond formed between us. To be honest, I actually did end up liking my doll.

This automatically prohibits me from owning a very large truck with aggressive bumper stickers, I know. But it did help make me into a boy who didn't react to infants as if they were tarantulas or time bombs. In fact, my parents recall me being very good with children, entirely comfortable picking them up, cuddling them, and burping them.

Sure, I had guns and army men and an uncle who taught me to sit on the retaining wall at the beach and rank chicks, but I also received a book called *Oh Boy! It's a Baby!*, which attempted to get boys excited about babysitting.

After giving me the book, my mother set up a trial run with a young neighborhood couple. They had a five-year-old son who liked to throw stuff and show people the contents of his nose. I was twelve at the time and still fully endorsed both activities, but my appreciation waned very quickly when I became responsible for boogers wiped in conspicuous places in the home.

The whole ordeal lasted less than a few hours. I doubt the parents actually trusted me with the safety of their only child. My mother probably paid them to sit in a van outside, where they nervously watched my progress on closed-circuit TV.

Nothing exciting happened. The five-year-old wanted to talk to me about airplanes — if I'd ever been on one, if I had peanuts, did I sit by the window, if I flew to see my grandpa like he did, if I thought he was the most annoying individual on the planet. I answered yes to all of his questions as I ate all of the family's food.

Babysitting was a girly thing to do and a bit embarrassing, but that wasn't the reason I decided that night it wasn't for me. I simply ran a cost-benefit analysis. The benefit was four bucks an hour. The cost was refraining from disposing of the child.

So because of the doll and my extensive babysitting career, I was a kinder, gentler sort of boy. A vague air of femininity surrounded me, of which I was blithely unaware. It took a half-flattened squirrel to make me realize I was different from the other boys.

Four of us were riding our bikes down the alley behind our grocery store when Geoff Mason came across it. Geoff was a nasty brute of a kid with freckles, a weight problem, and a case of chips on both shoulders. He was what happens when former high school football stars start copulating but don't stop drinking. He and I spent our preteen years getting into fistfights after school. But on this particular day we were friends — or were faking it to each other's satisfaction so that we could ride bikes together.

"Holy *shit!*" he yelled, stopping his bike with a sideways skid. "Look at *that!*"

He pointed to what appeared to be 50 percent of Bullwinkle's little buddy. Its back half had been quite literally flattened to the pavement, the fresh victim of a car tire. The squirrel was trembling but still alive. The images of its little life were flashing before its frightened eyes — *tree, acorn, grass, acorn, acorn, tree, grass, acorn, acorn, TOYOTA!*

"Whooooaah," said Tim Campbell, thoughtfully. Tim was a hybrid — half nice kid, half tough. He cut other kids with smart-ass remarks, but mostly he played well with others. Still, he had an older brother who made high school kids bleed, so the threat of violence was always nearby.

Completing the circle were A.J. and I. We were good mama's boys who occasionally knocked on our elderly neighbor's door to pet her lap dog. We were wussies.

"Dude, it's totally dying. This is awesome!" Geoff announced, as if the squirrel had just thrown a touchdown to an open receiver.

"Man, look at the back of it — it's fucking *flat*," Tim observed. "Bitchin'."

Ever since I can remember, I've felt an unnaturally close connection to animals. In the TV show *Lassie*, a young, nerdy farmboy could have a conversation with his collie. That was impressive. But I could look at a dog and tell you the contents of its soul.

I wanted to peel the squirrel from the pavement, put it in a cute little sling, and nurture it back to life. It would never be able to walk again, but it would learn to suckle from a bottle while I said, "Oh, thirsty squirrel. It's okay, Daddy's here."

"Let's kill it!" Geoff said.

"What?!" I stammered. "No, man. C'mon. Leave it alone. It's already dying."

Geoff and Tim were already rummaging through the bushes for rocks. They found a couple each and hurled them at the squirrel's head. As each stone zipped past its head, the squirrel became more panicked.

"C'mon, you guys! Stop!" I yelled. "Seriously!"

"Don't be such a pussy, Troy," Tim said. "You'd rather let it die slowly? The thing's in pain. We're putting it out of its misery."

I knew he was right. Unbearable pain was probably the only thing keeping the poor animal alive. But I couldn't do it. In situations that call for sheer, brute manhood, my first instinct is to empathize. I would have been the world's worst soldier. Upon encountering a raging enemy on the battlefield, I'd say, "Whoa there, man. It's okay. Let's talk about why you're so angry." And then he would stab me in the face.

The squirrel looked deep into my soul. Its eyes said, *It's okay, brother Troy. Thank you for your kindness. Now go. Go into this world and make more wussies.* So I hopped on my bike and pedaled away. I cried all the way home, knowing that a cute squirrel's head had just exploded, or was about to.

Because of all this, I have grown into what some people call a metrosexual. The word came into vogue as a means of describing the new breed of men who are in touch with their feelings and are helping America rekindle its love affair with moisturizer. A metrosexual doesn't grunt or fart unless he's sleeping. A metrosexual never sees Sally Struthers on TV talking about starving kids in Africa and thinks, *Fat cow.* A metrosexual dresses well, wears cologne, and manscapes — meaning he grooms his body hair and doesn't let his eyebrows grow until they meet at the nose and form an unholy alliance. Basically, metrosexuals are the new generation of wussies raised by Gloria Fucking Steinem.

I'm only part metrosexual, actually. I have the emotions down — I can sit with a group of women and talk openly about feelings of physical inadequacy. I can hug another man without feeling the need to beat him. Occasionally I go with friends to gay bars, and I don't spend the entire night maintaining postural rigor mortis.

But I'm also a slob. This garners metrosexual demerits. My apartment hosts a broad array of molds, and I don't own a pair of nail clippers. I appreciate a good camel toe. The Lifetime channel activates my gag reflex.

Still, because of my vaguely effete personality, I am occasionally mistaken for an honest-to-goodness gay man.

I once worked on a fine dining boat that served candle-lit dinners while cruising the San Diego harbor. I started out as a waiter but quickly rose to manager — despite being an awful waiter who couldn't up-sell guests on a $12 shrimp cocktail. I also drank on the job, stole a bottle of wine every shift, and slept with all the trainees who didn't have enough self-esteem to reject me. Not exactly management material.

Regardless, I was promoted. I thought it strange until my supervisor took me out to celebrate. After praising my people skills and college education, she — very visibly a lesbian — asked, "Okay, so I have to know. We've all been talking about this. Are you . . . *in the family?*"

Having enough gay friends at this point, I knew what she was asking. Think of it as gay vernacular for "Do you appreciate fine art and cruise for cock on weekends?"

She didn't care if I couldn't organize shift schedules or stuffed inventory down my pants. As long as I might be involved in a same-sex adoption case in the future, I was on the fast track.

"Nope, I'm a big, fat straight man," I replied.

"Really? . . . No offense, I just thought . . . huh." She gave me a look that said *It's okay, denial's a tough drug to kick.*

The situation worsened at my next job. I hosted a pre-game TV show for the San Diego Padres, a professional baseball team. The athletes aren't the chest-pounding gorilla-men many expect them to be. In fact, most of them have soft, gentle personalities that come from years of being on display wearing uniforms that are essentially ballet tights. The male fans, however, all seem to be compensating for small penises by pretending they're seconds away from a street fight. I didn't realize I stuck out in this crowd until I met the daughter of the team owner.

"Hey, Jennifer," I said to her in the dugout before a game one day, "I don't think we've met yet. I'm Troy Johnson. I host a new TV show for the team."

"Oh, I know who you are. You're kinda funny — in a dorky way. These are my nieces," she said, pointing to the two young girls next to her. They were stunningly beautiful teenagers nearing the age of consent.

"This is Don't Touch," she said with a smile, "and this is Jailbait."

This was my place of business, so I wanted to set the record straight. I wasn't here to pick up chicks.

"Thanks for the warning, but I don't think my girl-friend would appreciate if I asked for their phone numbers," I said.

"*Girlfriend?*" she said with a quizzical stare. "Really? I thought for *sure* you were gay."

"No, no, no," I said with a forced smile. "Not last time I checked. But I do wear makeup to work."

I am such a dork.

I wasn't embarrassed about being taken for gay. I was embarrassed because I'm a straight man — which meant I was doing a very poor job of acting like one.

At that exact moment, the gayest man associated with professional sports appeared, as if on cue. An usher at the ballpark, Larry had flaming red hair, wore eyeliner, and spoke with a lisp so perfectly gay that it could have been used to teach other gays. Between innings, he endeared himself to the fans by talking very loud in an exaggerated, flamboyant manner about trivial things. He was the Padres token homosexual.

"Now *Larry*," I said to Jennifer under my breath, "I'm pretty sure *he's* gay."

She glared at me as if I'd just made a statement about black people and fried chicken.

"Not that there's anything wrong with that, of course," I fumbled. Which just made me look like a bigot without enough gumption to stick to my bigotry. It was too late — her eyes said *homophobe.*

So I did what I always do in these situations. I outed my mother. "My gaydar is pretty fine-tuned," I said. "I grew up with a gay parent."

"Ahh . . . that makes sense," she replied, suggesting she understood my plight perfectly, that having a lesbian mom had blurred my own sense of sexuality.

This is my way. Because I grew up in the gay culture, I'm very comfortable joking about homosexuality. If someone thinks my jokes contain malice, I assure them I'm not a homophobe by outing Mom. It is my "get out of awkward social situations free" card. It's also my way of exacting revenge for having to deal with Tattle Dyke all those years.

Being mistaken for a gay man isn't so bad. But being hit on really challenges your comfort level. Gay men often stop and want to know what sort of styling product I have in my hair — because "it really shapes it nicely." When they realize I'm not going to punch them, they bite their bottom lips and coyly say something along the lines of, "You're *cute.*"

I have a little speech for this that's really quite effective.

"Oh, thanks," I'll say. "I appreciate it. Kinda makes my day, actually. But, alas, I'm a big fat straight guy."

I say the last line with a sigh and a shrug, as though I consider my heterosexuality a handicap, like impotence. I imply that if it weren't for my desire to stick my head between women's breasts and shake it around, the two of us might get to know each other better under the supervision

45

of a sommelier. Both the gay man and I leave feeling better about ourselves. The man with fabulous hair (me) turned him down only because I am burdened by my need to breed. And I am reassured that someone finds me attractive. This method has worked on almost everyone — except Tiny Russian Man.

I had gone to 7-Eleven to get a cup of coffee that tasted like vanilla-flavored armpits. My ex-wife and I lived in Hillcrest, San Diego's gay community, because it had better restaurants. The theater screened movies in which the plotlines didn't hinge on J-Lo's ass. All around, it just had a cleaner, hipper vibe.

Sidebar: Men, if women treat you as though you have a visible herpes sore, spend a year living in a gayborhood. You will be hit on like the girl in a frat house with a T-shirt that reads "I take the morning-after pill!" Gay men are still men. And men, no matter which way they swing, want to bed everyone. Even Gloria Steinem. A quick cheat sheet:

New York City: Chelsea

L.A.: West Hollywood

Boston: South End

D.C.: Dupont Circle

San Francisco: The Castro

Chicago: Boystown

Houston: Montrose

Phoenix: Encanto

Philadelphia: Washington Square West

San Diego: Hillcrest

Seattle: Capitol Hill

Dallas: Turtle Creek

Detroit: Ferndale

Tiny Russian Man was eyeing me as I poured my vanilla-flavored armpits into a non-recyclable cup. My convenience store was this man's single's club. Cranky from a dangerous lack of caffeine, I pretended that pushing the button on a coffee machine required intense concentration. He pulled up to the dispenser next to me and stared directly into my ear for ten seconds. I wasn't in the mood, but I was going to have to recite my speech and pretend to care.

He sized me up from shoes to crotch before saying, "You are just wonderful." I had bed head, bags under my eyes that Louis Vuitton could sponsor, and my breath smelled like a bar rag. This guy would fuck a fence post if it held still long enough.

"Oh thanks, I appreciate it. Kinda makes my day, actually," I said. "But alas" — *shrug* — "I'm a big fat straight guy."

I thought he was going to throw coffee on me. I realized instantly that I had no business buying vanilla-flavored armpits in the gay part of town.

"You're *straight*?!" he demanded. "Well that's just a *joke*! You're gonna wake up one day and realize what you've been missing!" He tossed his own half-full cup of armpits in the trash as he stormed off.

As I waited in line to pay for my caffeine, he approached me yet again. Apparently our encounter wasn't over. He studied my ear again until I finally turned. He made a lewd circle with his forefinger and thumb and presented it to me. In a voice loud enough so that the entire store could hear, asked, "Have you ever had a nice, tight butthole?"

"No, I haven't," I said, wearily. "I'm sure it's nice. It's just not for me."

He stormed out of the store without buying a thing. Giving the universal hand signal for "tight butthole" must have given him a sense of closure.

It's hard to say who made me such a sensitive male and a gay magnet — the feminist mom or the lesbian mom. Although I will say this: you can be a woman without ever burning a single bra, but you cannot be a lesbian without subscribing to *Ms.* magazine.

Chapter

6

Mother Theresa Has an Active Vagina

THE FIRST GUY I KNEW WHO FINGERED A GIRL was Ricky Sanders. Ricky was a good-looking Mexican kid who wore the right clothes and had a mole perfectly placed above his lip. He was Cindy Crawford with a penis.

Ricky and I played soccer together. I was better, and for a while scoring goals mattered more in our social pecking order than scoring girls. All that changed in the middle of dribbling exercises when Ricky held his middle digits up to Andy Newman's nose.

All of us were naive specks in the universe of sexuality. But we knew what it meant when some guy told you to smell his fingers. It meant you'd been to a magical place. Even if you still had a collection of Pez dispensers displayed prominently in your bedroom, you stood one step closer to

being a man. It also meant that "slut" was now an appropriate nickname for the girl who made your finger smell
funny. In turn, slut was defined as "a glorious female who
must be exalted by pointing and whispering when seen in
the cafeteria."

None of us on Ricky's team — it immediately became Ricky's team — had made it to second base. Most of
us were still in the batter's box of sexual experience, fiddling
with our packages. So Ricky became our Neil Armstrong.
His adventurous finger that smelled of woman was one
small step for him, one giant leap for our passing drills.

When Ricky spoke, we listened. This was the most
fascinating thing I'd ever heard in my life — including the
knowledge that cows played absolutely no part in the making of Cheez Whiz.

As humans, we love to hear about sex — unless it in-
volves our parents, or people who ride tour buses to casi-
nos. Or both. When someone refers to our parents doing it,
our faces contort as though we'd just found out the small
fried things we just ate once hung beneath a prized bull.

As the son of a gay parent, I can tell you why. Thinking about your parents having sex ruins what I like to call
the "adequately neutered caretaker" image.

As children, we are immensely vulnerable. In order to
grow into functional adults, we must depend wholly on
our parents. We must trust them with our lives — literally.
And in order to trust our parents fully, we need to know
they don't want to fuck us.

Some of the most mentally damaged people I know
were molested as children. A child could see Bambi ritually

tortured, find out one of the Wiggles was a cannibal, and see a Teletubby grilled to perfection and served on a bed of arugula. He still wouldn't be as messed up as a boy whose mother taught him how to unsnap her bra.

This is why in jail child molesters have the shelf life of yogurt. Even the scum of the earth — people who rob the elderly and sell crack cocaine to pregnant teenagers — think child molesters should die. Pacifists who hear that child molesters are killed in prison ask if you can e-mail them a link to the video.

I was never molested. My mother was always appropriately affectionate. But as soon as I found out she was gay, I figured that meant she might be capable of giving me a hand job.

What can I say — adolescent logic has never been praised for its rigor. But finding out your parent is queer automatically warps the adequately neutered caretaker image. You can't say someone is gay or homosexual without automatically thinking about that person in sexual terms. It's a little known offshoot of the pink elephants phenomenon.

Our brains have natural spam filters that prevent us from thinking about whether our parents like it on top or bottom. But as soon as you add the suffix -sexual to a defining characteristic of your parent, that filter is disabled. A healthy imagination becomes something you want to amputate like a gangrenous limb.

To make matters worse, the world has never been short on people who claim gays are the sort of people who have pictures of themselves doing inappropriate things with household appliances. In the early '80s, even prominent intellectuals were convinced that gays were two beers away from cruising schoolyards. I don't agree with this now, but I did as a kid — because adults told me so.

Before I found out my mother was gay, I thought about her having sex maybe once or twice. Each time I wanted to take my brain out of my head, place it in the sink, and scrub it with a wire brush. Once she was outed, I thought about my mother having sex at least once a day. The mental images of her bobbing between another woman's legs came with alarming regularity.

Retch.

My own thoughts stalked me. The last thing you want is to see your mother hug a female friend good-bye and imagine them slipping each other the tongue. But you do. The mind is treacherous like that. Kids of straight parents can't relate to this — and for good reason. They don't call them *straight* parents. They just call them parents. When someone asks, "What are your parents like? Who *are* they?" kids of straight parents don't think, *Well, Dad's a heterosexual.* They think, *Well, Dad's a plumber, and he likes beer and NASCAR.*

Whenever someone asked me to describe my mother, however, I thought about sex. Namely, her having sex. Because, judging by the reactions of, well, pretty much *everyone*, my mother's homosexuality was her dominant characteristic. More than rehabilitating quadriplegics or reading crime novels or even keeping score at baseball games.

Some people maintain that there is no difference between gay parents and straight parents. As long as they are still two loving, responsible individuals, a parent's sexuality doesn't affect the parent–child relationship, they say.

Bullshit.

Maybe if the family in question lives on the Island of Gay, where everyone is gay and has been since the gay dinosaurs died. Or if the entire family is on such a high dosage of meds that they all simply forget to think about sex. And even then.

Both family models have their shortcomings. Both gays and straights are capable of raising children who will win Nobel Prizes. And both are capable of raising children who will eventually sneak explosives into a Disney movie. But my issues with my gay parent were acutely sexual, so I forbade my mother from seeing me naked. My *mother* could. But my *lesbian mother* could not.

I locked the bathroom door from then on, which is why I remember so acutely the day I forgot to lock it. I wasn't big on showers. Not having hit puberty yet, my body seemed incapable of producing stench. Showers were for adults, whose bodies had blossomed into localized cells of olfactory terrorism. But occasionally I washed.

Somewhere in the middle of singing the second verse to the theme song of *T.J. Hooker*, I heard my mother trying to tell me something through the bathroom door. I fiddled with the soap in one of those unrinsable parts of my anatomy and screamed, "I can't hear you!"

She screamed louder. I made out the words, ". . . left your . . . floor . . . how many . . ."

She was probably reprimanding me for dropping my tennis bag and sweat suit smack dab in the middle of the living room. I'd been dumping my crap there for so long that I, like a dog, figured that space was mine. The onus was on others not to trip over my stuff. I pretended not to hear her, hoping by the time I got out that she'd be engrossed in an episode of *Cagney & Lacey* and had forgotten about it.

Then the unthinkable happened. The door opened. My mother was standing there, looking into the mirror, which reflected back at me in the shower.

I quickly covered my private parts with both hands. A single index finger would have sufficed.

"Mom! I'm naked! Get *out of here!*" I screamed.

Her face turned intensely red. She had entered annoyed, but now my embarrassment sparked her own. Which united with her annoyance to create a new and improved strain of anger.

"HOW MANY TIMES do I have to tell you to put your stuff in your room — NOT on the living room floor?!" she railed. "I have company coming over for dinner!"

"OKAY!" I screamed. "Now get out of here! Never come in the bathroom when I'm showering! *EVER!*"

And there it was — the first line in the sand. She didn't like it.

"Don't talk to me like that, young man," she snarled. "As long as you're living in my house, I will enter any room in my house whenever I want!"

With that, she shut the door.

"Bitch," I muttered.

I sat in the shower until my wrinkled skin looked like Henry Fonda's in *On Golden Pond.*

★   ★   ★

Later that night, my mother knocked on the door to my bedroom. I was still sulking. I was afraid to talk about this new situation. I was afraid I'd suffer from a momentary case of Tourette's syndrome and tell her how I really felt. (Not a onetime impulse, sadly. I've always feared, too, that in the middle of a Catholic wedding ceremony I'll stand up and scream, "Gimme the fucking wine! All of it! And Jesus Christ — all of you, wear rubbers!")

I was afraid I'd blurt out, "You can't see me naked because some people claim homosexuals are pervs. And I can't be totally sure that, along with gay sex, you wouldn't mind some son sex, too."

This was ridiculous, of course. My mother had never touched me inappropriately. In fact, when I was five years old she reprimanded me for trying to slip her some tongue. That day, I had been watching TV and witnessed two actors frenching. It was fascinating, like seeing two people touch their eyeballs together.

When my mother got home, I figured she would be my first tongue kiss. I started by chatting her up.

"Mom, I love you," I said sweetly.

"I love you, too, honey," she replied.

"Kiss me," I said, and she gave me a motherly peck on the lips.

"No, kiss me with your tongue," I said.

She flinched. Children are innocent and cute, but they can still give you the willies.

"No, Troy. Family members don't do that. That's for mommies and daddies. If a grown-up ever asks you to do that, you tell me, okay?"

"Okay," I said, wanting to tape shut my mouth until my tongue atrophied and dissolved.

"Has anyone ever asked you to do that?" she asked.

"No," I pouted, wanting to cry. "I saw it on the TV."

She chuckled that "poor little thing" chuckle and hugged me.

So Mom was no card-carrying NAWBLA pervert. She and Michael Jackson wouldn't share secrets in a cab. Deep in my heart I knew that. But between the kiss debacle and the shower fiasco, she'd become a homosexual.

"What, Mom? I'm studying," I said after she knocked, elongating my syllables so she knew I wasn't into whatever it was she was peddling.

She exercised her right to the power move and opened the door. My privacy was still on loan, after all.

"You can take a little break," she said. She was wearing that soft, concerned look that parents use when they're about to broach delicate subject matter. Like breaking the news that your sister's underwear is not appropriate headwear. Or, how pleased she was that I was getting acquainted with my "man-parts," but my teacher had asked that I refrain from doing it in class.

"Look, I'll tell you what," she said, sitting on the edge of my bed. "If you make a conscious effort to help out around the house — and that means not leaving your stuff in the middle of the living room floor — I promise never to walk into the bathroom when you're showering again."

"I'm not a kid anymore," I said with a subdued snort. "It was fine when I was a kid, because you're my mom. But I'm a man now."

She refrained from laughing aloud.

"I know you are." She nodded. "And a man deserves his privacy. But being a man also comes with responsibility. If you don't take the responsibility of cleaning up after yourself, that means you're still a boy."

Damn. She had cornered me with a domestic syllogism.

"All right," I moaned.

"I love you, you turkey," she said. My mother was a walking lexicon of terms of endearment. To most people, "turkey" was dinner. To my mother, it meant she wouldn't trade you in for a new microwave if the opportunity arose.

She leaned over and kissed me on the hairline, but I could feel the unspoken in the air. She wanted to know why I was acting as though our house was Eden and someone had made a great, big, juicy apple pie.

I didn't say that my knowledge of her sexuality had shrunk the comfort zone between us. I didn't tell her that it had charged the air in the house, like a theater pumping the smell of popcorn into the ventilation system. I didn't tell her that against my will some demented part of my brain was constantly flashing images of her doing lesbian things. I didn't tell her that on at least one occasion I had wondered whether, when cuddling me as a child, an inappropriate part of her had tingled.

Retch.

That my mother was completely comfortable with her naked body only exacerbated the problem. If my sister or I needed her, she had no problem inviting us into the bathroom while she sat on the toilet completely nude. She patiently answered our questions as if she were at her desk paying bills.

Now, even that behavior became suspect. Had she been baiting me? Sexual advances weren't often made while sitting on the john, but how was I to know?

One day I asked a friend, "Have you ever thought that maybe your mom wanted to have sex with you?" He looked at me as though I'd just told him that instead of eating my lunch like the rest of the kids, I inserted it rectally.

I didn't tell my mother any of the above because I knew that I was the delusional nutcase — not she. My mind was taking me wherever I didn't want to go on a regular basis.

To make matters worse, many of my friends were hitting puberty. Overnight, they became overly excitable, angry, confused people who might sexually assault fire hydrants or wipe out a family of five. I was sure my voice would crack soon enough, which would only add to this psychodrama playing out in my own head.

Chapter

7

God Hates Fags

WHEN I HEAR THE WORD *community*, my mother and her sisters come to mind. They are holding hands somewhere, singing songs about the need for strength while a few of them cry.

Unfortunately, that's not what the word meant for Rancho Bernardo Community Church, where I was chaptered and versed in the ways of Mr. Christ. Their definition of the word was more, "Brothers and sisters united against abortion, fags, and good music." In that order.

For example: these people hadn't heard that the scientific community officially declassified homosexuality as a disease in 1973. Even if they had, they'd have just seen it as further proof that Satan was an associate professor of temptation at Johns Hopkins University.

"You believe the news today, Joe?"

"What's that, Noah?"

"Some Harvard egghead thinks homos aren't diseased — and the rest of the so-called scientists *believed* him."

"Well, they obviously haven't seen the man-whores falling out of their cut-off jean shorts down at the park at night. I've driven by once or twice. Lost souls if I ever did see some. It's a disease, all right. One that leads to drug use and excessive finger snapping."

"Let's hope it never infects the people we love."

"God's love will serve as the antidote."

"Amen, Noah."

"Amen, brother Joseph."

Later that night, their wives would wonder why they were having uncharacteristically rough rumpy pumpy.

Meanwhile, my mother was popping an extra quarter into the tithe basket because she'd spent the entire sermon eyeing a plump lady in the front pew, wondering if she smelled nice.

One of the first songs I ever learned to sing was "Jesus Loves Me," and the empirical logic of the chorus went: "Jesus loves me, yes I know! 'Cause the Bible tells me so." It confirmed my mother's teachings. There were four things in this world that were never, ever wrong: the Bible, my parents, my teachers, and *Cagney and Lacey.* In that order.

The Bible doesn't feature any feel-good stories about gays. There was no homo at the Last Supper teaching the brutish apostles how properly to hold a wine goblet. When Jesus turned one fish into thousands, no tender man politely asked for low-fat lemon-dill sauce.

If these stories did exist, the transmission of the Bible erased them. Everyone agrees that the world's greatest carpenter said it was a good idea to be honest and nice and good. But nowhere does Jesus say it's okay for Roman soldiers to give each other blow jobs — despite what James Kirkup and Derek Jarman have to say on the matter.

I didn't have to go to church to learn that God hates fags, either. Orange juice commercials could have told me as much. Some of you know where I'm going with this. For the rest of you . . .

The 1970s were a boon for orange juice ads on TV. The best ads were for Florida-brand O.J. They were porn for people with a citrus fetish. In the commercials, dangerously happy Floridians engaged effortlessly in summery activities. Men played tennis or lawn sports in clean, white outfits while their women sunbathed blissfully nearby.

Penetrating these scenes were shots of juice spurting into and up from inside a glass — a cinematic device first pioneered, I believe, in the movie *Deep Throat*. The message was clear and well executed: O.J. was not only tasty and fortified with vitamin C, but it improved your backhand and inspired half-naked housewives to tan themselves in your presence.

The star of these commercials was the voice of Anita Bryant. She was a pop singer loved by Americans who were too white to understand what Tina Turner was saying. When Bryant sang "Breakfast without orange juice is like a day without sunshine," she soared. She may have had a great butt and a nice smile, but it was her musical talent that sealed her victory at the 1958 Miss Oklahoma beauty pageant.

Emboldened by her fame, Bryant thought it might be a nice idea to use her power for good. In 1977, Dade County, Florida, was about to pass a human rights ordinance that basically said you couldn't deny gays employment or tie them to fence posts. Shocked by such amoral politics, Bryant formed Save Our Children, a religious group that claimed homos were recruiting kids.

My favorite Bryant quote is a classic: "If gays are granted rights, next we'll have to give rights to prostitutes and to people who sleep with St. Bernards and to nail biters." A chronic nail biter myself, I'd like one day to be able to marry a girl with matching nubby fingertips, so I was all for it. Comparing my mother to people who used a lint roller to remove dog hair after sex, however, seemed a bit harsh.

But Bryant's plan worked. Dade County and the State of Florida eventually banned gays from adopting children. By 1994, New Hampshire followed suit — then Virginia, Arkansas, North Dakota, and Missouri. Although my home state of California had specific laws stating gays could adopt, the national consensus was that my mom wasn't really qualified to be my mom. She wasn't even qualified to save a crack baby from a childhood of dysfunctional foster care.

Someone shoved a pie in Bryant's face during one of her impassioned speeches. People even gave up drinking orange juice. Not one gay from Chelsea to the Castro ordered a mimosa during the late '70s.

As the years went on, more and more people on TV and in the newspapers told me about my mother's fate. Among the most famous was Pat Robertson. Robertson is the Howard Stern of Jesus TV, with fewer fart jokes but nearly as much power. He once ran for president. His budget plan probably called for killing all the gay people and selling off their expensive furniture to eliminate the deficit.

Robertson anchors a Jesus TV show called *The 700 Club.* He has said that embracing homosexuality could result in hurricanes, earthquakes, tornadoes, and "possibly a meteor." Every time you hug a gay person, you contribute to the skyrocketing premiums on home insurance. Tallying the hugs and assigning each their own tornado, I figure I was personally responsible for the ruin of a few thousand trailer parks.

Robertson also told me that my mother had such great lesbian sex on September 10, 2001, that it caused planes to steer into the World Trade Center the next morning. Clearly, whatever was happening behind her locked door offered a viable alternative to nuclear energy.

Another person eager to tell me about God's distaste for my mother was fundamentalist Baptist pastor Jerry Falwell. Most of the pastors who were against mom's kind were Baptist. Which really bummed me out, since Baptist churches had great music, with stomping and shouting and black people. The churches I attended had sad white folk who sang like Crystal Gayle — if she had a throat condition she was attempting to treat with Prozac.

Falwell and a chipper fellow named Robert Grant founded the conservative political action committee called the Moral Majority. When Metropolitan Community Churches started letting homos come openly to services,

Falwell showed his moral support by calling them "brute beasts" who were running "a vile and Satanic system."

But Falwell's greatest contribution to society was a hard-hitting report in his magazine *National Liberty Journal* that exposed the Teletubby named Tinky Winky as an ass bandit. The character was purple, carried a clutch purse, and had an inverted triangle on its head. I knew cartoons made me crave sugar-coated cereal, but I had no idea that Johnny Quest and Hadji were soft-selling me on boy-on-boy action.

Hell, even rock 'n' roll stars hated fags — especially Sebastian Bach. Bach fronted the 1980s hair-metal band Skid Row and had fabulous hair that flailed wildly when he sang on MTV. He wrote one of my all-time favorite songs — "I Remember You," a ballad about "writing love letters in the sand." But Bach was no fan of my mother. He is widely believed to be the first person to wear the inspirational T-shirt that read, "AIDS Kills Fags Dead." After Skid Row broke up, he landed the lead role in, ahem, a musical. *Jesus Christ Superstar.* Surprise, surprise.

The most outstanding member of the unofficial God Hates Fags Council, however, was Fred Phelps. Phelps was a pastor who taught that people who loved homos would be killed off by God, via comet or other fire-based phenomena. He showed up at the funeral of Matthew Shepard, a gay teenager beaten to death by bored high school kids. Some people brought roses. Phelps thoughtfully brought picket signs that read, "Matthew Shepard Rots in Hell."

Ironically, Phelps was the best thing ever to happen to gays who considered Jesus their homeboy. Robertson and

Falwell, though condemning my mother to eternal damnation, came off as likable people. Phelps, on the other hand, was a speed freak who sent his kids door-to-door to raise money for whiskey. He beat his wife, too, but at least she got off easier than the neighborhood dog, which Phelps shot for crapping on his lawn. He nearly ruined the image of religious homo-haters. Some suspect he was a member of the gay mafia working deep undercover.

For a while, I believed these people. I believed that I loved a woman who was going to hell. Then one Sunday Mom walked into my room wearing slippers instead of sensible dress shoes. "Why don't we watch the Chargers-Cowboys game on TV instead of going to church — would you like that?" she asked. It was as if someone had said, "You know, instead of taking out the trash, why don't we pour it on the living room floor and jump around in it?"

I *loved* the idea.

It wasn't long until we dedicated every Sunday to the San Diego Chargers. This was the early 1980s, when the team enjoyed a brief sabbatical from their title as Worst Football Team Ever. They had infinitely more flair than Jesus. Until then, Jesus had been the reason I owned a clip-on tie and my slick, parted hair smelled like Mom's spit. That year he became more of an acquaintance to whom we threw a shout-out to before passing the bacon.

As the year went on, I vaguely missed Jesus Trivia Joust and defiling various biblical characters with crayons. I even missed the old people in the congregation who smelled like earwax. No child — save future serial killers — digs church in the same way they dig, say, churros. But church had taught me the essentials of life: Don't lie. Don't cheat. Don't steal. Run like hell and pray your brains out if fireballs and a horn section appear in the sky.

Three years later, it clicked. My mother stopped going to church because she was making a run for it. The elders at Rancho Bernardo Community Church said that sexual deviants and sodomites were on God's hit list. What I hadn't realized was that they were talking about my mother. Quite a rude awakening. One day you're nodding along, going, "Yep, they're going to hell. Yep, them, too. Fry those suckers!" Then the next day it's "Yep, they're going, too — wait, what? Mom?"

The breakup was inevitable. Mom had birthed me and taken me to baseball games. Jesus just told me I couldn't do stuff. I had to let Jesus down easy. *Dude, it's not you, it's me.*

The surf was three feet and slightly choppy the day I asked my mom about the fate of her soul. We were driving to the beach in her Volkswagen Rabbit. It was a little hiccup of an automobile — big enough for a family of one and a half. That day I was the half. I was thirteen at the time, and we hadn't been to church in five years.

"Mom, can I ask you something?" I said, looking out the passenger window at the bigger, cooler cars passing us on the freeway.

"What's up, sport?" she said.

"Do you think you're going to hell?"

She let out an impressive chortle that only plus-sized women and lesbians can make. "What makes you ask that?" she replied.

"The Bible says being gay is a sin. And you're, y'know —" I paused. I could talk to my mother about "gays" as a general concept, but I had trouble directly attributing queerness to the woman from whom I inherited half my DNA.

"You know . . . *you're* gay." I said this as if I was telling her there was a snot glob dangling from her right nostril. Again, it was my way.

"Ooohhhhhhh," she said. "Well, that's a toughie. No one really knows the answer to that, hon."

This pissed me off. For years, I'd had television rights revoked for doing things that supposedly bummed out Jesus. I never had the option of saying, "But Mom, did Jesus ever actually say it's a sin to throw eggs at moving cars?"

"You told me the Bible was our rule book," I said. "And from what I can tell, being gay is breaking a pretty big one."

My mother sighed. "Well, the Bible is a good book, Troy, a *guide* for life, but it was also written two thousand years ago. There are things in the Bible that were written for that time in history. For instance, there's a part that says women need to wear hats in church. Do you think God would punish me for not wearing a hat?"

"No."

"Exactly. Back then it wasn't acceptable for a woman to show her hair. It was considered scandalous. Now it's not scandalous — it's just hair."

Hmmmmm. She was right. While my mother's straight, black bowl broke a few hairdressing rules, it wasn't on the same page as murder or porking your neighbor's wife.

"The story about Sodom and Gomorrah — that's the one you're referring to, right?"

"Yeah," I said, totally unsure. I just knew somewhere the Bible said, *Fags are Satan's kindling*, or something to that effect.

"Well, that was during a time when men and women needed to hunt and fish and take care of the household. The death rate was really high among infants, so any sexual relationship that didn't produce a baby was considered wrong. They needed workers in order to survive. And a loving relationship between two women or two men obviously didn't produce children."

Workers? That was officially the most disturbing version of human reproduction I had ever heard. Our species had survived because our ancestors screwed for employees.

"Nowadays the opposite is true," she continued. "There are too many people on the planet. We don't need workers. We need *fewer* people, because half the people are starving. So, as far as I believe, that guideline no longer applies."

Wow. Now, not only was my mother's sexuality okay — but by being gay she was saving a starving third world child from having to eat bugs and drink his own urine. She had just justified what a friend of mine calls Cafeteria Christianity — picking and choosing the stuff you want and discarding the rest. Cafeteria Christianity is a form of religiosity where you can watch Demi Moore in *Striptease* — even the DVD bonus footage — and sleep well at night because you believe you'll be in heaven one day with your grandparents and the family dog.

"You have to take it in context, I guess is what I'm saying," she said, sliding her '70s tortoise-shell glasses back up her nose and changing lanes. "That's just my opinion. Religion is different for everyone. What's important is your own personal walk with God."

I sat silently for a second, letting this newly imparted wisdom sink in as I nodded my head and looked out the window at the other, better cars.

At the time, I didn't care much about walking with God. I wouldn't have even taken him up on free movie tickets. But I had received what small set of morals I had from Christianity. I still flipped through the Bible now and again when I was utterly confused.

For instance: If I was considering whether or not to steal money from our family piggy bank — a huge metal Quaker Oats can — I would flip open the Bible to a random page. There, the Epistle of James asked me, "Can a fig tree, my brethren, yield olives, or a grapevine figs?"

Not knowing what the fuck that meant, I just took the quarters out of the can anyway.

"Well, that's good. I don't want you going to hell," I said, clutching her hand. No matter how mortified I was by

Mom's gayness, I loved her. Even if she was wrong, I figured Jesus could pop her open like an old Chevy and fix
her once she arrived.

I hadn't felt such relief since my sister moved out of
the house. I now knew Mom wasn't polishing her hand-
basket, and that was good enough for me. Plus, if a homosexual could feel safe, then surely a callous punk who had
pantsed Lena Reynolds in front of thirty of her middle
school peers wouldn't be Satanic chum, either. The Bible
was fairly mum on "pantsing." No one picketed pantsers.

Still, religion can form a huge obstacle to coming to
terms with a gay parent. Salvation is not like speed
dating — though if it were, more people might give it a
try. It's never easy to say, "Oh, Jesus doesn't dig homos?
Well then forget him. Who else we got? Buddha? Krishna?
Bueller? Anyone?"

Chapter

8

You're Such a Fag

PUBLIC SCHOOL IS HELL. It's especially tough for kids of gays or students who know enough about themselves to know that they're gay.

At least this is how it was during my years there, which ended in 1991. I haven't gone back since. Police tend to frown on thirty-somethings doing any sort of social networking among large groups of teens. But back when I was in hell, the ultimate insult was to suggest that matching genitalia inspires a person to slow dance.

Most kids learn homophobia before they learn what a homosexual is. Responsible parents eventually decide it's time to talk to little Johnny about bigotry. But they usually don't do so until Johnny's a teenager, when it's too late.

"Johnny, we think you're old enough now, and it's time you learned about what a homosexual is," a mother will say.

Johnny will look at her the same way children always do, as if their parents have been living in a hermetically sealed box for the last decade. "Which kind?" Johnny will reply. "Lesbos, fags, or trannies?"

A thousand kids on playgrounds across America have made little Johnny very comfy with the word *fag* long before his parents think he's ready to learn about such an adult topic. When I was in high school, there was no Gay Straight Alliance, in which gay kids hung with future breeders, both realizing they're not that different from each other. After all, everyone appreciates *Raiders of the Lost Ark* and enumerates the ways in which parents have totally, completely ruined their lives.

Gay advocates like to describe ours as a culture of hate. They're right. But it doesn't start that way. Among kids, it's not hate; it's more a culture of *ick*. If given enough positive feedback for the creative usage of the word fag, childhood teasing then develops into something more sinister.

When I was a kid, asserting that someone was gay easily outweighed calling them a dickface. Although offensive, anyone in the general vicinity could see clearly that you did not have a penis where your nose should be. When someone calls you an ass muncher, however, no one can immediately prove that you do not, indeed, go directly home from school to munch ass.

Calling another child a queer also cuts straight to the core of who they are. No children (and few adults) are evolved to a point where "lover of pointillism" or "connoisseur of Jean-Claude Van Damme's lesser-known art films" forms part of their identity. So being a boy or a girl is all we have. And, without treading too far into normative gender roles, to suggest that we're boys who like boys or girls who like girls is to suggest we're not *real* boys or girls after all.

Actually, these insults are primarily — though not exclusively — wielded by boys. Girls are simply nicer humans, and lesbians are tougher to detect when they're young. If a girl prefers to wear baseball caps and hang out with boys, we allow her to be a tomboy, assuming she has two older brothers and developed substantial biceps because they were necessary for her survival.

Girls are also socialized to be affectionate with one another. They hug, kiss, hold hands, and — well — act gay. Boys, on the other hand, learn from day one that expressing physical affection for each other is worse than French-kissing your grandmother. If two boys shake hands for longer than two seconds, one of the two will back away instinctively and hit the other one in the face. The other one will deck him back with equal affection. Then they laugh off their pain and call some adjacent boy a fag.

It is the way.

It's especially tough on males because Dick Van Dyke, Sylvester Stallone, and the inventory manager at Toys "R" Us have taught us that only good, manly heterosexual boys grow into real men — real men whom *People* magazine exalts in its list of the Hottest Men You'd Love to Sleep With But Never Will Because You're . . . You.

In the 1980s, we knew that fag was a bad word, so we rarely if ever used it within earshot of adult women —

because, again, adult women are nicer humans — but we used it liberally in front of adult males. In fact, I often used it to bond with them. Usually it was because the men were the ones who taught us the word. At the time, the word fag was equivalent to using the word nigger in the Deep South in the 1950s. Everyone knew it wasn't kind, but it hadn't yet become socially reprehensible.

Calling other kids fags also proved so effective because there weren't any truly cool gay celebrities. If Ellen De-Generes had made the cover of *Time* or starred in American Express commercials, *lesbo* wouldn't have been such an insult. A sense of gay esteem would have whittled down the vitriol of the word.

Most of the famous gay people were all dead. Plus, they had done boring things in life like write books (Radclyffe Hall, Walt Whitman, Oscar Wilde, Virginia Woolf). Sure, Herman Melville was reportedly gay when he penned *Moby-Dick*, but what did that do for me? He wasn't throwing great parties with Sean Connery and Goldie Hawn. He would never co-host *Yo! MTV Raps!*

Gay musicians and artists had visibility, but adults teach us that artists are crazy. Andy Warhol creeped people out until he was shot. Melissa Etheridge made folk music that required special LGBT training to appreciate. Freddie Mercury had bad teeth, wore white lycra jumpsuits, and died of AIDS.

To prove to each other that we weren't gay, we bonded by picking on boys who might be. If none was readily available, we picked a kid we didn't like and used him as proxy. Lucky for us, we had Jeff Spencer.

★　　★　　★

Jeff Spencer was living, breathing evidence for the nature side of the Nurture vs. Nature debate. In the District Court of Homosexuality, the defense attorneys for Nature could have paraded him out at age five. "I present to the court little Jeffrey Spencer. Note the limp wrists. Jeffrey, please try to maintain a rigid posture. See! A physical impossibility!"

As if trying to leave absolutely no doubt, Jeff actually skipped. Real boys run as though trying to create potholes with every step. Jeff landed lightly, delicately on each foot, hands flopping to and fro. He had no interest in associating with boys. We were dirty, foul creatures who couldn't appreciate the proper application of eye shadow — which Jeff had learned in middle school.

If someone did something we disliked — such as, refusing to destroy private property for kicks — we would simply call him Jeff Spencer. That is, until the day my mother shot me *the look*.

I was fourteen years old. My mother had been out for four years. My best friend A.J. and I had spent the day at the mall picking up chicks. Our strategy was to walk around the mall, pointing out good-looking girls, and never say a single word to them. Talking *about* talking to them was a necessary training exercise, though, ranking just above passionately tongue-kissing the back of your hand.

Finally, chickless but feeling somehow closer to manhood, we rendezvoused with my mother for a ride home.

"Can you believe Jeff Spencer was there?" I said in the car.

"I know. Probably shopping for a new skirt," A.J. chuckled.

My mother's attention shifted, eyeing A.J. in the rearview mirror.

"Who's Jeff Spencer?" she asked with a fake smile and transparent curiosity.

"He's just a kid from school," I said.

"He's a total fag," A.J. snickered under his breath.

"*Total* fag." I laughed.

"Troy *Michael*!" my mother barked out of the side of her mouth.

I crumbled the way only mothers can make you crumble. But here was a chance for my mother to cement her ruse as a straight woman — a ruse I'd been encouraging for a few years. If she let this go in front of A.J., he wouldn't suspect a thing. I hoped.

"*What*, Mom? He *is* a total fag," I replied, baiting her.

She glared at A.J. in the rearview mirror and then back at me. Her eyebrows lifted as if to say, *Oh yeah? You wanna play this game? You're on.*

"Would you like me to explain to A.J. why that's not very nice?" she threatened.

I realized instantly what she was implying. She was going to out herself to A.J. right there and then.

"No," I grunted. We rode home the rest of the way in silence.

A.J. was my best friend — I told him everything. But I never thought for a second to tell him my mom was gay. Because my mom was his mom. He spent half his life in my house, and I spent half at his. Telling him might scare him off.

Not long after the Jeff Spencer incident, I finally sat him down. My mother, acting erratically courageous, could no longer be trusted to conceal our secret. I wanted him to hear the words from me so that I could let him know that in no way was I fond of this development.

"Man, I gotta tell you something," I said after we had just finished doing bench presses on the exercise equipment in my room. The moment was so manly it would take a whole pride parade to overcome the machismo. "You have to promise me you will never, ever tell anyone. Not your parents, not your girlfriend, no one."

"Sure, man — I swear."

"Well, my mom is . . . Fuck, this is hard to say. Okay . . . My mom's a . . . lesbian."

Confusion makes people look like pug dogs. A.J.'s forehead furled, and his face sucked inward. "Whoa . . . *Really?*" he said.

"Yeah," I concurred. "Whoa."

"Like a *real* lesbian? So her and Louise —?"

"Yep. You have to promise me that you will never, ever tell anyone, no matter how much I piss you off."

"You have my word, man. That's just so . . . *weird.*"

"No shit," I said.

Then, simply, he concluded, "But, hey, she's still cool."

And that was it. We pumped more iron. A.J. was perplexed, but not nearly as grossed out as I expected. Emboldened by his response, I told Tim Campbell a week later.

"Duh," he said. He seemed more offended that I thought he was stupid enough not to know this already. (*Was it that obvious?*)

For the remainder of my high school years, I only told select close friends or women who had let me sleep with them and with whom I planned to stay longer than a week. My sister told only her best friend, Jodi. To this day she can count on one hand the people with whom she has shared this information.

For four years, my mother had heard my sister and me use the word fag as if it were a common adjective, even though we knew she was a "fag" herself. I had partially used it to help her throw off the scent — or so I told myself at the time. If she played along, no one would suspect her. It was an inconsideration bordering on hate. I would never have thought about using the word "nigger" in A.J.'s house. That was unequivocally wrong. But playfully bashing gays — even to their face — still hovered in the gray area.

Of course, being black and being gay are very different things. For one, scientists haven't determined whether anyone's truly *born* gay. Nor do religious leaders claim that black people cause God to throw a tantrum of tornados (anymore, at least). But my best friend and my mother shared a similar distinction — they represented the two greatest bigot-magnets in twentieth-century America.

Our generosity with the word fag helped keep my mother in the closet as long as she was. After my sister found the "Gay Rodeo!" clipping, she asked my father if Mom was gay. Not wanting any part of that conversation, my father said he wasn't sure and suggested Kim ask the source.

My sister did, and my mother lied to her face.

During therapy, my mom explained that we had scared her deep into the closet — past the hamper, past the shoes, into the mental crawl space behind the insulation. She also revealed that she had proposed to Tattle Dyke that they explain their relationship to my sister and me. Tattle Dyke apparently vetoed the idea because we might tell her own kids. How's that for irony?

Because we called people we didn't like fags and things we didn't like gay, my mother really thought her kids hated homos. She didn't want to be the one screaming "I speak Yiddish!" in a house full of little Nazis.

After that day in the car, I never used the word fag again in front of my mother. I'd love to say I stopped using it altogether, but there were still a few years to go before I figured out bigotry wasn't my best attribute.

Chapter

9

Coital Overcompensation

MEN LIKE TO REFER TO WAKING UP WITH an erection as having "morning wood," which sounds like an expensive cologne. Using the accepted nomenclature, I am convinced I had birth wood. Blame it on the process. When you're born, the doctor or wet nurse or taxi driver smacks you. Unless your mother's been drinking Schlitz the entire term, this undoubtedly causes your newborn eyes to pop open, if for no other reason than to convey an inaugural version of *"What the fuck?!"*

When I was born, the doctor must have turned me around before his AMA-sanctioned flogging. I'm convinced my first impression of this world was a vagina. Granted, it was my mother's, but ownership is unimportant. Vagina guided a large portion of my decisions from then on. Had he been more of a planner, the doctor would have propped a nice photo of Harvard over my mother's exhausted lady parts.

By the time I reached kindergarten, I had already spent quality time in my family's giant toy box with the cute black girl from my neighborhood. We cuddled and pressed our lips together until we realized it didn't get any better than that. But still, I was advanced.

In kindergarten I initiated my first mass-scale womanizing. At a sleek three feet, ten inches tall, I became founding father of an epic game of kissing tag. My chapter at Sunset Hills Elementary School was exemplary. It boasted so many members that eventually administrative intervention was necessary. I was the Jimmy Hoffa of kissing tag.

Kissing tag was simple. At recess, boys ran like hell and girls chased them. If a girl caught you, she kissed you — a form of torture akin to spooning with a leper. Properly played, no physical contact should ever occur in this game. Boys are genetically designed to win foot races. If we stand still for more than five minutes, our legs start to shake like an alcoholic at a wine tasting. We chase dogs. We bound up descending escalators. We run to honor running.

Girls, however, aren't as interested in ricocheting like pinballs through the world. They're sensualists. They pause and absorb. They like to consider how a flower relates to their inner child and other associated hooey. To compound their gender-induced lethargy, girls wear cute shoes made of shiny leather and buckles and bows. These shoes click on asphalt and aren't properly engineered for speed.

Among boys, running shoes are standard issue. Mothers who make their sons wear dress shoes might as well shoot them in the knees.

This is why kissing tag was a perfect, innocent game: naturally curious children get to pretend they're interested in physical contact. Fleet-footed boys so fear being kissed that they never get caught. Kids chase each other fruitlessly until they're too tired to make farting noises with their armpits during math class.

Come recess time, we all lined up and walked toward the playground. At about thirty feet, we were treading a brisk pace. At ten feet, we were performing an early form of power walking, an exercise activity that makes suburban housewives look like crack-addled ducks.

The faces of the five-year-old boys around me lit up and flushed with a combination of excitement, embarrassment, and fear. The girls huddled, pointed to the cute boys and conspired. Though not OshKosh catalogue–worthy, I wouldn't have been part of a class-action lawsuit against Ugly Stick, Inc., either.

As soon as we hit grass, the boys fled in a confused, lopsided herd. Think drunk hyenas. The girls daintily gave chase, their arms bent and pulled toward their bodies. Think Tyrannosaurus rexes in pigtails.

Occasionally an athletic girl grabbed a fingerful of a boy's shirtsleeve — usually because the boy was bored and trying to increase the drama. If not for the drama, we could all just go back to segregating the playground according to gender, confident that interaction with the other sex led to head lice and leprosy. No boy was ever caught or kissed. Except one.

I was widely considered to be the worst kissing tag player in the annals of kissing tag history. I returned to class reeking of girl spit and strawberry lip gloss. I had an uncontrollable tripping problem. I excelled in every other sport — four-square, kickball, heads-up 7-up — but when it came to kissing tag, I always stumbled. And I stayed right where I was. Tripping *was* victory.

I pretended to guard my face as girls swarmed me with their tiny, fluttering lips. I twisted and turned my head, making all the usual sounds of disgust. But everywhere I turned a lovely new set of girl lips wet my cheeks. Occasionally, the confusion resulted in a moment of lip-on-lip action, and a warmth rushed over me — like the first time I saw my sister cry.

Having exacted their punishment, the girls scampered away to catch the other boys. It was then — and only then — that I would spring to my feet and beat a hasty retreat. I easily outran the girls with the buckled pink shoes and joined my fellow men.

"Whoa, we didn't think you were gonna make it!" they'd breathlessly stammer. "Let's go!"

Fools. Within minutes I was planning my next fall.

It was heaven until the day the girls realized that I was a faker, tripping on nonexistent gopher holes. So began the days of sadness. The girls slowly, silently shunned me from my own game.

My ruse was up the day I stumbled to the ground and

only chubby-fingered Lisa Stowell lumbered in my direction. Her breath smelled like tuna fish, and snot had dried around her nostrils. A vision, to be sure. I sprang to my feet and ran like the wind so I wouldn't have to sock her.

Luckily, it was only a matter of days before a mother asked her precious five-year-old daughter, "What did you do at school today?" To which her little flower gleefully replied, "I kissed boys!" That is how freeway accidents happen. It's not cell phones or old people. It's a five-year-old girl in the backseat of a minivan telling her mother that she sucked face at recess.

It took only one mother to accuse the administration of facilitating a "Golem-like atmosphere," and kissing tag entered a long and dark period of prohibition. Its entrepreneurial spirit didn't resurface until the advent of Truth or Dare.

My depression didn't last long, which is one of the great things about being a child. A newborn can go from "I need some motherfucking milk now, woman!" to "Ooh, pretty carpet" in three seconds. The older we get, the greater our ability to stew in our own sadness, to analyze its many levels of suck. Because I was five when banned from kissing tag, it was only a day or so before I discovered that spitting skyward and catching it in my mouth brought equal happiness.

Despite my trailblazing expeditions into inter-gender territory, I was the last of my friends to get laid. Blame it on the unexpected delay of my pubic shipment. I was what they call a late bloomer. It wouldn't have been so bad if I could have kept it hidden, but, thanks to the public school system and their annoying adherence to health codes, I was exposed on a daily basis. Every day after gym class I was forced to realize how very sad my little hairless penis was.

After running around on the blacktop, shooting hoops, and playing flag football at Black Mountain Middle School, three coaches herded us into a long shower stall like lambs to the slaughter: Mr. Blalock, Mr. Resnick, and Mr. Houle. Houle kept the decomposing bodies of twelve-year-old boys in his locker, we had heard.

These meaty, muscled P.E. coaches reeked of cologne acquired from the automotive section at Sears. And they were all obviously gay. We concluded this because every day they walked down the aisles of lockers and yelled, "Thirty seconds to hit the shower! And I don't want to see ANY TOWELS!"

For those of us still lacking grass on the playing field, this was torture on a par with someone finding out that once — just once — you had dry-humped your sister's Cabbage Patch doll.

It wouldn't have been so bad if there weren't people like Matt Rodriguez. At age eleven, he was hung like a prize stallion. He was a fat kid. We, on the other hand, were hairless and cute. Girls had crushes on us. But his grossly developed manhood was his trump card. And we bowed before its mighty shadow.

He dropped his towel and paraded around like a family

terrier with its favorite chew toy. He lathered up his manhood and just kept lathering. I'm pretty sure that he never washed any other portion of his body. You could smell his armpits if he sat behind you in math class, but he had the cleanest penis in the world.

Actually, penises were what we had. Matt Castillo had a dick. A friend told me about his college-age brother who was apparently the proud owner of the ultimate classification: a cock.

My father assured me that all Johnson men were late bloomers, but my little pleasure patch was so barren I thought maybe my manhood hadn't been planted at all.

"Trust me, bud. I know it doesn't seem like it now," he told me one day when I asked how long he had to wait, "but you've got plenty of time."

"Doesn't feel like it," I sulked, depressed that I was fourteen and deformed. "Feels like I'm the only one at the keg party drinking near-beer."

"And that's a good thing, seeing as how you *shouldn't be drinking at all*." He smiled. "Plus, look at the bright side —"

"What bright side? That I can't get a girl pregnant and continue our proud line of late bloomers?"

Dad chuckled. Apparently he appreciated a good underdeveloped dick joke. "Well, there's that, and you'll never have to watch chick flicks and pretend you don't understand the lead character's struggle with body image."

"Actually, I think I could."

"Hmm, good point. Well, at least you've got nice breasts," he said, pinching my nipple through my shirt.

"Screw off."

I was allowed to cuss at my father. When I was younger, I had anger issues. One minute I was peacefully making things out of Play-Doh, and the next I was throwing wild punches at my father for suggesting I make something other than a miniature penis.

I raged.

My family nicknamed me The Hulk, and frequently paraphrased the TV show's famous line: "He's cute, but you wouldn't like him when he's angry."

The family psychologist believed my anger stemmed from my parents' divorcing when I was three. The crack in the family structure had created two versions of me: the dutiful son and the hellion who locked himself in the bathroom with scissors and banged on the toilet for hours so that it ricocheted through the plumbing and drove people insane.

I still cite the source as Scrappy, who completely assassinated the original zeitgeist of *Scooby Doo*.

Regardless, the psychologist suggested that my father allow me to let me call him a rat bastard son of a bitch whenever the need arose. It was exorcism by potty mouth. The poor man agreed to it.

Offers for sex at a young age further aggravated my late development. A girl named Mandy Davis made it very clear that she was willing to help me, at age twelve, escape the loser fraternity of virgins. She let me fondle her breasts.

But reciprocity terrified me. One day on the school bus, Mandy had talked about another boy, snickering when she reported he had an "ocean dick." I had no idea what that meant. Maybe it was like one of those sea sponges —

slimy, cylindrical things that shoot spermatozoa without warning and for no apparent reason.

"What's that?" I asked her.

She held up her pinky, then curled it a bit so that it was even smaller. She gave a look that said, *Yeah, that small.* This girl couldn't do basic math, but she had already developed her own measurement system for male genitalia. No child left behind, indeed.

"No *way*," I said, feigning disbelief that a teenager could be so physically inadequate. Meanwhile, the nub between my legs was still a mushroom cap in search of a stem.

Of course, she eventually tried to go there. I had been kneading her breasts like pizza dough, when, most likely just to stop the abuse, she attempted to slip her hand beneath the waistline of my corduroys. My whole body froze. I dropped her breasts and grabbed her wrist — speechless.

After all, what do you say when you're stiff-arming someone who's given you free reign of her young body? I thought about something adult like, "Terribly sorry, I've already got three kids in other states. Child support really takes a chunk out of my allowance. Gonna keep it in my pants for a while."

What actually came out of my mouth was, *"Eaahh-hhnnaaahhhwhhoa."* She persisted, playfully trying to break free and penetrate my no-fly zone for a full thirty seconds before finally giving up. Then she pouted, gazing at me with the look of someone who'd been unequivocally gypped. I had broken the unspoken code of copping feels.

Embarrassed, I slunk out of the bushes. She followed.

We rejoined our friends. They had all seen us go into the grove, so they had the expectant faces that Navy men get when their drunk pal emerges from a red-lit building.

"*Soooooo?*" said Mandy's older sister, demanding an oral report on behalf of the group. Julie was the madame of the Davis siblings. Having broken in all of her own orifices by the time she could drive, she now pimped for her sibling. I had deeply, religiously appreciated that fact right up until the point Mandy tried to discover my deep, bald secret.

"I've got an injury," I blurted. *Oh my God. Did I just say that out loud?*

For a second, everyone looked at me with horror, as if my penis were in a sling. Maybe I was one of those kids who had tried mixing peanut butter and the family dog, and things had gone terribly wrong.

"Surfing," I said, attempting to clarify. Perplexed and probably realizing that I had a wee willy, my friends mercifully changed the subject. Mandy, though, was peering at my crotch, approximating the sea level of my package.

When I was thirteen, Robin Rathburn — rumored to have "showed and telled" her double-D boobs in second grade — wrapped her arms around my waist while we were walking through a haunted house at a county fair. I seized up as if my cellmate had just stuck a shank in my back and said something about taking our relationship to the next level. I ran.

It wasn't that I didn't want to flop up and down on top of Robin on her parents' couch. I wanted that more than anything in the world, but I knew that bringing my penis to a sexual encounter was like bringing a copy of *Aladdin* to a bachelor party.

My underdevelopment was immortalized my freshman year in high school — with the help of a girl in my English class named Shane Sterling, who had brilliant blue eyes and porcelain white skin. Time came around for the annual Sadie Hawkins Dance, in which, in an electrifying reversal of gender roles, girls asked the boys out.

Born with an innate distaste for rules, I walked right up to Shane one day in English class and asked her to the dance. She was cornered. She had probably been daydreaming about whom she wanted to ask — the captain of the water polo team or Chris Cooper, who was the sort of guy who could model sunglasses in surf magazines.

And now I, a hairless mutant with braces and satellite dishes for ears, had thrown a wrench in her plans.

She told me she'd think about it, which meant: *As soon as class is over, I'm running to my friends to beg them for a good excuse.*

"Just tell him you've already asked someone," one girl might say.

"Tell him you're grounded that weekend — he won't get another date, so he'll never know," another would offer.

Then a girl with a cigarette dangling from her lips and a vagina stretched to the size of a cantaloupe would groan, "Ask to see his ocean dick."

To my complete shock and horror, Shane accepted my invitation. Word spread throughout the school like crabs in a commune. "Shane Sterling is going to the dance with — are you ready for this? — *Troy Johnson!*"

"The one who looks like an eight-year-old? No *way*! I wonder if he'll take her doorbell ditching afterward."

I had officially scored a date with the best-looking freshman in school. And there would be photos to prove it.

Of course, Shane didn't consider it a date. It was a shrewd plan on her part. If boys like Chris Cooper were the alpha-male pit bulls of teenage sexuality, I was a neutered purse dog. If I made any advances, Shane could extend her arm and put her hand against my forehead as I ran in place and made kissy faces with my eyes closed.

We spent the whole dance sitting at the nerds' table. Shane's friends necked with the popular boys at a table on the other side of the gymnasium, a safe distance from any dweeb contagion that might spread their way. Occasionally they waved to her and giggled. Meanwhile, she and I were engaged in a deep conversation that went something like this:

Me: "Wow, those kids really are dancing."

Her: "Yep."

Me: "Wow."

Her: "Uh huh."

Shane later became a bikini model for ads that appeared in national surf magazines for which I wrote. She also became one of Bob Barker's Beauties on the game show *The Price Is Right*. She married a sun-blond high school classmate who owned a surf shop in San Diego and they reportedly gave birth to runway models.

Somewhere in a closet, though, she has the same photo I do. There she is — porcelain skin, blue eyes, puffy blue dress — timidly embracing me, as required by the unwritten rules that govern high school dance photos.

I am smiling so wide that every metal wire and bracket on my teeth is visibly gleaming under the studio lights. The highest pinnacle of my hair — plastered skyward in the shape of a wave — reaches her chin. She looks like my chaperone, assigned to make sure I didn't drink too much punch before bedtime.

It was one of the proudest and most embarrassing nights of my life.

Less than a year later came the most magnificent pee I have ever experienced. I mindlessly aimed like I had thousands of times before, trying to land the stream of pee in the middle of the water in the bowl, which would make the splash resonate deeply. Anyone hearing me from outside the door would thereby assume that large noises came from large things. The rigors of adolescent logic hard at work again.

Only this time, I discovered the single greatest hair known to man. My first pubic hair.

It looked more like a nose hair, small but conspicuous. Stopping midstream to analyze and honor its arrival, I seriously considered snipping it off and putting it in a special box.

After a few moments of hesitation, I lovingly squeezed it between my thumb and my forefinger, massaging it as though it might be capable of ejaculation. My bladder yielded to the thrilling magnitude of the moment.

Glorious months followed. Hair after hair sprouted to give moral support to my penis, which was growing noticeably larger. A two-finger pee turned into three. A three-finger pee turned into four. A four — well, let's just say I was pleased. Many kids felt embarrassed when their voices cracked, deepening with the process of puberty. I purposefully called attention to myself during those moments, as if to say, *That's right, ladies, it's arrived.*

I was also desperate. I was fifteen years old, and all of my friends had lost their virginity. I was the lone virgin among us.

Girls were always talking about waiting until they were in love. I didn't want love. I wanted a semi-operational vagina attached to a girl who didn't mind if I told every single one of my friends. I was ready to throw myself at the first willing, female participant, excluding the acutely repulsive or those limited by a full body cast. And even then.

The day I finally got laid was as pedestrian as my requirements for laying someone. I was walking home from school to my friend Jason's house to smoke his dad's cigarettes or listen to Depeche Mode albums. A young Hispanic girl named Mariana joined us. She was a year younger and could have qualified as a midget, but she had genetically inflated lips and double-D breasts.

Halfway to Jason's house, Mariana coyly said, "Troy, keep walking. I need to talk to Jason." She had been flirting with me, so I thought maybe she was going to tell Jason that she thought I was cute, that she wanted to share a pizza.

After their brief tête-à-tête, Jason ran to catch up with me. "Hey, Mariana wants to know if you've ever had sex."

"Of course," I responded, as though it were a ludicrous

question. No boy admits he's a virgin unless asked in the presence of a handgun. If the condition lasted until age eighteen, then he pretends his inability to boink is a personal choice. Which is much the same as bartenders with an IQ of 12 saying they've "chosen not to be manipulated by the corporate structure." Most boys act as though they received sex for Christmas sometime shortly after kindergarten.

"Dude, I think this might be your day," Jason said.

And there it was. All I had to do was not suffer a bout of uncontrollable flatulence and I would enter Jason's house a boy and emerge a man. *Oh God, what did I have for lunch?* I don't think I said another word to Mariana until we found ourselves in Jason's bedroom, kissing each other the same way starving people attack small fruit. It was barely 3:30 in the afternoon, and I was ripping off her clothes. At approximately 3:33, I was having sex. At approximately 3:35, my universe exploded.

It took less time than it takes to make mac 'n' cheese, and then I rolled over speechless. Older people often say thank you to a partner after great sex. Then they cuddle and pretend they mean it. I, on the other hand, tossed on my clothes. I would love to say that I spooned Mariana and talked about how eventually we'd be named cutest couple in the high school yearbook, but I was a base shallow teenager who viewed this sexual encounter not as a shared act of intimacy between two humans but as a rite of passage. Her body had been a way to belong.

Even more important than becoming a man was what sex made me. It made me a heterosexual. Which is not a homosexual.

"I need to check on Jason," I told her, as if my friend would swallow cleaning products if not frequently monitored. Timed correctly, I figured I had roughly two and a half minutes to tell him every single detail before Mariana could get dressed. Additional time could be used to embellish.

I had never ejaculated before this day. I tell friends this story now and they look at me as though I tried to run for president before learning to add and subtract. (For which there is now a winning precedent, but that's another book.) Fact is, I had heard only vague rumors about male ejaculation and how it was this indescribable high that could result in tiny, unwanted humans.

I thought about this later that night as I took a shower, and logic descended as it rarely had in my life. That extra-special moment between minutes two and three of sex with Mariana had yielded what adults called sperm. And sperm at my age wasn't good. It meant dropping out of school and working the rest of your life as a flower delivery guy whose only goal was to have cable TV.

So I decided to try it out. I masturbated for the first time in my life *after* having unprotected sex. Genius, I know. Sure enough, within minutes I felt the same *holyshitgoddamntractorpull* feeling that I had felt with Mariana, and then four million sperm cells leapt to their death down the shower drain.

Mental images of dirty diapers and sing-alongs with Big Bird assaulted me. I had seriously screwed up. Since I knew even less about human reproduction than I knew about sex, I was sure that I was a brand-new papa. So I did the most reasonable thing I could imagine: I called Mariana to have an open discussion about the possible repercussions of our actions.

"I think I came in you," I told her.

"Uh, yeah," she said flatly.

"You could get *pregnant.*"

"Yeah, it's not good," she said.

"So that got me thinking — and I think the only responsible thing is to break up." As if we had been an item.

I figured that if a woman walked in the opposite direction and a child happened to fall out of her, then that child was the world's, not mine. My first instinct as a biological man was grotesquely typical. You didn't embrace hardship. You embraced another girl and prayed that the first one would become a nun and take a vow of silence.

Mariana got her period a week later. In true high school fashion, she told Jason, who told me. I was so relieved that I wanted to celebrate by having sex again. Which we did. This time I lasted approximately 45 seconds longer than the first time, due to my newfound comfort zone. We didn't use a condom, but that didn't faze me. My sperm was on my side. It had street smarts. It was *selective.*

I also reasoned that since my first pubic hair had arrived a half-decade late, my sperm probably wouldn't ripen until a few years down the road. Not until I had a diversified investment portfolio would it finally yield a child — so fuck away!

Mariana ended up being my first friend with benefits. No matter how crappy the day — whether the jocks had teased me, my sister had beaten me, or NBC had canceled

Growing Pains — I could almost always spend the after-school, pre-parent hours at Mariana's washing our blues away with awkward, radically brief sex.

Once my zipper opened, it stayed open. Sex with girls was a way to prove that I wouldn't wear women's dresses one day. Unless, of course, an attractive woman asked me to do so as a prelude to sex.

Chapter

10

Natural Born Delinquent

WHEN I WAS FIFTEEN, I was sent to Charter Hospital, an in-patient treatment center for troubled kids and those who are cranky because their crack cocaine has been taken from them. It was not, as I told my fellow inmates, "as a safety precaution to protect me from my sister."

Many events led to my incarceration, but first and fore-most was that I had discovered in myself a natural born talent for mischief. My parents loved me and made sure I didn't have access to amyl nitrate, but for some reason that only God and Dr. Phil have the power to discern, I was attracted to trouble — especially if trouble entailed breaking stuff.

When I was nine, a construction company started building houses in our canyon. My best friend A.J. and I had played for years in that canyon. Illegal aliens made their homes there. While they were gone during the day aerating suburban lawns, we co-opted their plywood dwellings as our forts.

And now haggard men on tractors were leveling our dirt hills of joy. In their place rose terra-cotta stucco boxes where boring people would live. They were shit brown, the official color of California suburbia. They looked like bad wedding cakes.

So we decided to destroy them. It wasn't as noble as eco-terrorism, in which white college dropouts with dreadlocks set fire to anything touched by John Deere. It was ego-terrorism — and ours were crushed.

We started from the safety of A.J.'s backyard, hurling his father's collection of jazz 45s. Very few people know this, but small vinyl records take to flight surprisingly well. They soared hundreds of yards and landed in the sparkling new pools and shattered the brand-new windows. That didn't dissuade the builders, though. Construction continued. So we accepted the challenge and snuck down into the canyon for point-blank destruction.

A.J. and I assumed strategic spots — like a big clearing where you could see us from every direction. From there, we gathered rocks and executed our attack. We stood about 100 feet from our targets and fired round after round, pausing long enough to make sure we hadn't been detected. We took turns, devised a scoring system, and high-fived. The sound of broken glass was our applause. A rock that broke a small hole was a smattering. One that brought down the whole pane was a standing O. Within weeks, we had reduced nearly thirty windows to shards.

We thought we had permanently altered the construction schedule. Somewhere, we imagined an oafish man with jaundice sweat stains and steak sandwiches on his breath was hovering over a set of blueprints and production reports.

"We were going to have these units finished by December!" he'd bark to no one in particular, slamming his fists down on a drafting table. "But these attacks on our infrastructure have put us behind. *WAY behind!* Inform the crew that we're pulling out. The underwriter feels it's too risky."

Since we were sure that armed men would be rapelling from helicopters to hunt us down, we feared for our lives. As such, we only worked up the nerve to break windows every few days. We spread it out so that their counter-intelligence agents couldn't establish a pattern for the crimes.

In reality, we were merely an annoyance. The workers probably just hoped they didn't get thwacked by an errant throw. Of course, that's exactly what happened.

A.J. and I were near construction lines collecting rocks when we heard voices a hundred or so yards away. We couldn't see over the mounds of dirt, but we could tell it was the workers. The brilliance usually associated with severe head trauma struck us: *Breaking windows is fun, but it's not getting us anywhere or resulting in a good chase. Change of plans.*

This was dangerous. This was good. We stood there for a full five minutes gathering our courage. Finally, I reared back and lobbed a test shot in the direction of the voices.

THWACK!

It was the unmistakable sound of a rock landing squarely on a hard hat. It was the sound of success on the *very first shot!* A.J. and I looked at each other with the most excitement and fear we'd had since the day Chrissy Wellington discovered cutoff jean shorts.

"Aaahhhhhhhhhhhhhhhhhh!!!!!!!!" bellowed a deep voice in the distance.

We turned in the direction of the scream just as a massive, uncoordinated construction worker flew over a dirt hill. He had a hand to his hard hat. He ran like a pack mule wearing swim fins, but he was surprisingly quick.

A.J. took off up the hill. He was the fastest kid in the neighborhood, firsthand evidence of why there are no white people left in professional sports.

I froze. This man's gnarled, angry face neutralized my fight-or-flight response.

I just stood there looking — and feeling — as if I'd freshly wet myself. I began to hyperventilate. He ran full speed until he reached me, grabbing the front of my shirt with both fists.

"YOU LITTLE SHIT! YOU THINK THROWING ROCKS AT PEOPLE IS FUNNY?! YOU CAN KILL SOMEONE! YOU COULD'VE KILLED ME!!!"

Until this point, A.J. and I had been playing the role of macho soldier types waging war against evil people who hated the places where children play. That self-image crumbled the moment I felt my tear glands contract.

"YEAH, THAT'S RIGHT! YOU GO AHEAD AND CRY, YOU LITTLE SHIT!" the man yelled into my ear. Budweiser vapor had never flown from an orifice at such speeds.

"WE KNOW YOU'RE THE ONE THAT'S BEEN

BREAKING THE WINDOWS! WHAT DO YOU THINK YOUR DAD'S GONNA SAY ABOUT THAT WHEN I TELL HIM?!"

About twenty seconds later, I was still shaking violently, making noises people usually reserve for death and orgasms.

"HEY! HEY!... Hey... BUDDY. Stop it, now, c'mon. Take a breath, for chrissakes." His voice softened. A nail gunner with beer breath found standing over the dead body of a nine-year-old is hard to defend in court.

"You're gonna be okay. You're in big trouble, but no one's gonna hurt you."

By then, the other construction workers were huddling around us, wondering whether their friend had beat me and if it felt nice. Eventually my breathing slowed and my panic attack downgraded to a massive freakout.

"Okay, bud. It's gonna be okay," said the only man wearing a shirt with a collar. "Now let's pay a visit to your mother." He grabbed my shirtsleeve from the other man and told the others to get back to work as we headed up the hill to our neighborhood.

The foreman led me up the walkway to the house and knocked on the door.

"Uh, 'scuse me . . . uh, *ma'am*? Is this . . . well, obviously . . . I mean, is this your *son*?"

Words failed him. He must have thought I was adopted — or albino — because the woman at the door was black.

"No, it's not," said A.J.'s mother. "But I know where I can find her. What seems to be the problem?"

The foreman explained the events that had led to our

little rendezvous. Mrs. Payne loved me like her own son, but she also knew I might end up in a penitentiary. At various points, she had banned A.J. from hanging out with me, but she also knew it was fruitless. A.J. and I were inseparable.

"ARCHIE ANDERSON PAYNE JUNIOR! GET YOUR LITTLE BUTT OVER HERE . . . *NOW!*"

A.J. slunk up to his mother's side, head down, and the foreman smiled. It was true — I had the loyalty of a common prostitute. I had hoped that Mrs. Payne would just deal with it and not tell my mother. No such luck. At least I could call A.J. for the next few weeks and moan, "Man, being grounded sucks, doesn't it?"

A year after the rock-throwing incident, the police and I became acquainted.

While most kids saw nightfall as a time to eat dinner and do homework, I saw it as natural camouflage that allowed me to terrorize families who were eating dinner and doing homework.

My friends and I tossed so many eggs at random houses that our parents must have thought we were on high-protein diets. Once we antagonized a neighbor so badly he chased us — with a baseball bat. When he brought me home by the collar and a Louisville Slugger in his hand, there was only one thing to do. I fell to the floor, writhed on the carpet, and told my mother he had hit me. An hour later, police literally jumped out of the bushes and tackled him to the ground outside his home while his wife and six-year-old son watched in horror. My mother decided not to press charges when emergency room doctors suggested the red welt on my back didn't "appear to be from blunt trauma, but from irritation — possibly prolonged rubbing." They were right.

The first gun drawn on me, however, was during the most innocuous childhood prank: doorbell ditching. The single mother A.J. and I ditched at ten on a Friday night apparently had seen one too many horror movies. She was convinced the phantom bell ringer was a man with a hockey mask and a chainsaw.

After we rang the poor woman's doorbell a third time and ran to our hiding spot in the bushes, a man walked up to her door. It was Policeman Dan.

Policeman Dan was our neighbor. He was a strange fellow who had a "psych. eval." file separated into chapters. After years of looking at crime scene photos, Dan thought, *Hey, these would make great party favors!* He broke them out whenever my father and stepmother went over for a visit.

"Oh, oh, oh! Look at *this* one!" he'd say, producing a black-and-white image of what had once been a human body. "It's a *floater,*" he explained. "Perps dispose of bodies in rivers and they come out looking like they're gonna pop. You gotta be careful when you pick 'em up. Their skin slides right off."

Getting a call about a psycho killer ringing doorbells doubtless made Policeman Dan's Friday night. After a brief conversation with the terrified mother, he turned to the darkness of the street and yelled, "Okay, whoever you are, this is no longer a prank. It's now *official police business.*"

As we watched from the bushes, he pulled back the

top of his sweat suit so that the handle of his gun was visible. He put his hand to it. "If you show yourselves right now, we can handle this thing without having to go down to the station," he said.

About to crap ourselves, A.J. and I slowly crawled out of the bushes with our hands up.

Policeman Dan let his shirt fall back over his gun and shook his head. "Troy, what in GOD'S NAME do you think you doing? You think this is *funny?* You're having fun scaring the bejesus out of a mother who's alone with her children?"

A common question. From the time I was five, countless adults had very angrily asked for my philosophy on humor.

"No, I don't think it's funny," I said. "At least not now."

"I want you to apologize to and tell her you'll never do it again. Which you won't, right?"

I apologized, adequately shamed.

Policeman Dan said good night to the woman, calling her "ma'am" and acting as though he had just caught the Nicaraguan drug dealers who had kidnapped and julienned her husband.

As he led us back toward my father's house, I pointed to the lump at Policeman Dan's waistline and mouthed to A.J., *"Did you see that?"*

Of course A.J. had. Cops shoot black people for jaywalking or driving nice cars. His fear dwarfed mine.

When we reached my father's house, I started up the walkway.

"Hold it," Dan said. "This way, you two."

He motioned toward his house, and we followed him

through the front door into his living room. I was sure he was about to pull out photos of teenage boys whose faces had been blown off for toilet-papering people's yards.

He instructed us to sit on his couch as he headed to the phone and dialed my father's number. "Rich? Well, I have two suspects in custody — one is an African-American male, age ten. The other is a Caucasian male, also age ten. Does this sound familiar?" He said this without a trace of jest. He had known A.J. and me for years. He had shared finger foods with my stepmother and laughed as he explained that "exit wounds are *so much bigger* than entry wounds, which is all *most* civilians get to see." And he couldn't just say, "Hey, Rich — your fuck-up son was doorbell ditching the single broad down the street. Come get him."

My father retrieved us, serious and grave, assuring Policeman Dan that in no way did the Johnson family endorse doorbell ditching. He spent the next eighteen Thanksgivings laughing beer through his nose while recounting that phone call.

I was eleven the next time Policeman Dan and I did business. My friends and I had decided to celebrate someone's birthday by breaking all the windows of the trailers at Sunset Hills Elementary School. We had been forced into those dwellings the year before. They had piss-poor air conditioning and smelled like carpet glue. The floors creaked like old hookers whenever you got out of your seat when you weren't supposed to.

It was personal.

One by one, we took turns throwing rocks from forty

yards away, trying to break the small windows on the trailer doors. It would have been much more effective to stand point-blank, true, but that would have drastically reduced the fun quotient, and doing so would have made us common vandals. Our destructive behavior was more than that; it was a test of physical prowess.

"Ohhhhhhh," we would groan in unison whenever someone hit the door frame, barely missing. "Next!"

Pete, the birthday boy, initially refused to participate. So we enacted initiation rule #3521-P and called him a pussy. Nowadays, if someone called me a pussy in an effort to get me to break the law, I would assure said someone he was right. But when you're eleven years old, it's an affront to your basic existence, so Pete joined in.

After we broke four windows and smashed a few lightbulbs on the premises, we huddled and took a vow of silence. From what I can tell, pacts among preteen boys are like wedding vows — they make you feel safe, but only the religious and the really ugly intend to keep them.

The following Monday at school, administrators held a witch hunt to find the vandals. During an especially brutal round of interrogation, Pete the birthday pussy caved and ratted on us all. I imagine the questioning went something like this:

"Pete, we want you to take your time and think hard. Do you know anything about —"

"YES! I DID IT. WE ALL DID IT — KEVIN, BRIAN, VINCE, A.J., TROY. OH, GOD, PLEASE DON'T TELL MY MOM! AND I LOOKED AT MY

TEACHER'S BREASTS AS SHE BENT OVER IN CLASS TODAY. I SAW NIPPLE. OH GOD . . ."

Children aren't hard to crack. We tell adults all they want to know because they're taller and their shoes are tied.

The Sunset Hills stoning led to three days of suspension. Which, when you think about it, is a ridiculous punishment. Under this disciplinary brain trust, kids who hate school are "punished" by being forced not to go to school. And since America is the sort of place where you need seven incomes to pay the mortgage, few parents have the leisure to stay home.

So the message is: "Oh, now you've done it. For napalming the cafeteria, we're going to make you sit home and watch cartoons all day. *That'll* teach you."

My father was smart enough to realize this, so he brainstormed a way to scare me straight. He considered putting me in juvenile hall for a few days so I could get a taste of where I seemed destined to end up. But doing so would have exposed me to the really bad kids, who would teach me how to cut the cocaine with baking soda so I could keep a little for myself. Instead, he called Policeman Dan.

Dad picked me up on my first day of suspension, and told me we were "going for a little ride." Dad's idea of discipline was not allowing me to super-size my Happy Meal, so I assumed we were going for a milk shake right up until we pulled into the police station.

There, a cop led us to a corner office. Dan greeted us and asked my father to wait outside. By removing my father from the room, he took away my psychological woobie, and the bastard knew it.

Policeman Dan told me to sit in the chair on the other side of his desk. He sat silently for a good ten seconds then sighed heavily. "Well, Troy, you've really done it this time," he said. He shuffled through some papers as if my name might be on them. (It wasn't.) "The police are aware of your actions. We got a call from Sunset Hills. You're now on the same watch list as the boy who tried to set the principal's car on fire. Remember him?" Bullshit, of course, but I was too scared to debate.

Then he gave the most effective speech anyone has ever given me in my life.

"Troy, this was your world when you were born," he said, holding his hands far apart from each other. Then he moved his hands closer together. "This is your world now. If you do something like this again, your world will be *this* —" He slammed his hands shut. I flinched.

"Your world will be gone, Troy, because you will be in jail. No friends, no freedom. All your friends will be doing whatever they want to do — going out with girls, surfing, having a good time. But you will be behind bars. I've seen kids like you before, and trust me — you're one step away from going to jail for a long, long time. You still have a choice. This," he said, spreading his arms back out wide. "Or . . . *THIS*," as he slammed them together again.

Images of unwanted advances by a gang of men in orange jumpsuits assaulted me. I asked to be excused and went out to my father. My rock-throwing days had ended. Policeman Dan was now my Yogi, and Dad took me for a milk shake.

Chapter

11

Puberty Kills

ROCK THROWING AND HOOKY PAVED the primrose path to my incarceration in the chicken coop for kids, but pubic hair pushed me over the edge.

Puberty isn't kind. There is a ritual in Tijuana bars where a man sneaks up behind you with drain cleaner in a Tequila bottle. He pours it into your mouth, grabs your face, shakes your head, and blows a rape whistle directly into your ear. Your brain slams back and forth against the inside of your skull, and by the time he's done you're not sure if you're amazingly drunk or legally dead. If you added electroshock, Viagra, and backne to this mix, you have an idea of how I felt when hormones threw a frat party in my body.

Kids undergoing puberty should be kept under constant supervision, just in case they decide to frott dangerous objects or throw produce at the mail carrier. My mother —

again, an overworked lesbian whose lifestyle wasn't allowed in her own home — couldn't provide such supervision.

My anger issues peaked at this point in my life. Quality time with Mom consisted of my standing at the end of the hall, fifty feet away from her in her bedroom, yelling at the top of my lungs how much I hated her. This pastime might have continued uninterrupted had I not been such a drama queen and held a steak knife to my gut.

It was the predawn morning after a great party my friends and I had thrown beneath a freeway overpass. I was *severely* late for curfew on a night I was spending with my dad, and my dad was waiting up. This wasn't a problem — he had been doing it for months but couldn't catch me.

Whenever I was late, my father would prop open his bedroom door, which had a clear view of the front door. So I snuck to the rear of the house, dropped to all fours and shimmied through the doggie door — which had been built for our shitsu. It seemed impossible, but if I stuck my hands through first and scooted forward inch by inch, I could make it. Then I would sleep on the couch, so I didn't have to pass my father's bedroom.

On the night in question, however, it didn't work so well. Despite being advertised as a way to keep off unwanted extra pounds, light beer had added a few to my frame. I was halfway through the door when my hips jammed. I pushed and pushed until they were so stuck that I couldn't even back out.

I slept there that night, the top half of my body warm, the bottom half cold and damp with dew. My only hope was that the hilarity of the situation would make my father forget his anger when he eventually found me.

The next morning my father came downstairs to make breakfast. As he rounded the corner, a bowl of peach oatmeal in his hands, he spotted me and did a double take — then laughed harder than I'd ever seen him laugh.

"Hey Cin!" he yelled, choking on his oatmeal. "Come here! You *gotta* see this!"

They cracked jokes and let me stay there as they finished breakfast. Then Dad pulled me out and got serious. "You're grounded, buddy."

This was a rarity in the Johnson household. I had a date that night with the cousin of a friend. She had big breasts, sex in her eyes, and she was in San Diego for one night only. And he knew this.

I was livid. I screamed. I threatened to drop out of school and run away. It didn't faze him.

An hour passed, and he didn't budge. Drastic measures were necessary. I went downstairs and grabbed a steak knife. I listened for footsteps on the stairs, and I stuck the knife against my gut. My stepmother turned the corner and saw me. The only time I have seen her so concerned was when she met my half sister's new Russian boyfriend, who was wearing a T-shirt that read, "Cocaine!"

I wasn't going to kill myself, but I had heard that sticking sharp things against one of your major organs got stuff done.

The next day in my room I was doing what I usually

did during this period of my life — lying in the dark, looking at the dark, becoming one with the dark. There was a
knock on my door.

"Fuck off," I moaned.

"Troy," said a man's voice that I didn't recognize. "It's
Officer Nest from the San Diego Police Department. Would
you mind coming out here for a minute?" I could hear a
dispatcher on his walkie-talkie speaking a crackly, numeri-
cal language.

My brain quickly scanned itself for recent illegal activities. None registered. I went to my bedroom window,
figuring I'd jump out and escape through the yard. I pulled
up the blinds to see a cop standing outside. I was trapped. I
walked to the door, wondering if my cellmate would be
large, and if he preferred top or bottom.

Officer Nest hadn't drawn his gun. He had a nice,
warm countenance, like TV cops who have to tell someone
their spouse was ground to bits by a wood chipper. My
mother and father were standing behind him. Together.

"Troy, your parents have asked me to come talk to
you," the officer said. "They're worried about you. I understand you've talked about hurting yourself?"

"Yeah, so what. That's not a crime, is it?" I asked.

"No, you're not in trouble," the officer said. A wave of
relief washed over me. This was just about the *steak knife*? I
wasn't going to jail because I'd shoplifted beer from the
liquor store? Great news.

"Why don't we go talk in the living room."

Waiting in the living room was another man — an
EMT, with a toolbox. Maybe they were going to take out

113

my bad heart and put in a better one, possibly a transplant from a well-adjusted kid who died tragically erecting houses for the poor in Mexico.

"Troy, your parents have asked us to do an intervention," he said. "Do you know what that is?"

Uh-oh.

For the next five minutes, my mother cried, and my father told me they were worried sick. Static voices crackled through the walkie-talkies.

"Troy, we'd like to take you down to a treatment center, just so they can run some tests and make sure you're okay," the EMT explained. "Would you mind coming with me?"

Didn't seem like I had a choice. And home wasn't my favorite place, anyway, so why not?

The EMT led me to an ambulance parked outside. I climbed into the back with the officer, and we drove off. I had no idea that I was about to spend a month with kids who made my life seem like Ward Cleaver's wet dream.

Chapter

12

Charter: Not a Story About Boats and Exotic Seafaring

THE TREATMENT CENTER LOOKED like an office building — as if these "tests" would be administered by people in power suits. They would poke and prod me around a large mahogany table topped with croissants, bottled water, and juice. If only.

As we piled out of the ambulance, Officer Nest grabbed my arm. His grip activated my problem with authority, and I freed myself with a quick roll of the shoulder. "Hey now, bud," he said. "Okay, you can walk on your own. But if you run, we're gonna have problems."

I didn't run. I hated my home life. I didn't have a ride home, and I was fascinated. Charter Hospital had its own ambulance. Police officers brought people here. *Beats the shit out of daytime TV,* I thought.

We walked through the automatic sliding doors. A lone woman sat in the waiting room. She looked like what would happen if scientists fused a young mother and a corpse, then managed to get it to walk around and look nervous. Bags hung under her eyes, and she anxiously twisted the strap on her purse. My fascination gave way to a slow, escalating panic.

The girl at the desk who greeted us was pretty and perky, the sort of perky you practice in the face of adversity. She was young, probably a junior in college who interned at Charter during the day and had ravenous, promiscuous sex at night.

"Troy here needs to be admitted," said Officer Nest.

"Well hello, Troy," the perky girl said. "From Mount Carmel High, right? I had friends who went there."

"Yeah," I said flatly. I wasn't here to chat. This girl knew where I went to high school. She knew my name, my address, my everything.

"Why don't you take a seat right over there, and I'll have a nurse come right out."

A few minutes later the nurse opened an inner door; she was a very large black woman who could have led the NFL in sacks. "I'll take if from here, Officer. Thank you. Troy? Nice to meet you. I'm Lorine. Come with me, honey."

She put her hand on my shoulder and led me to a room just behind the nurses' station. It had no furniture save for a single pad on the floor — the type they use to train gymnasts. The room was bare — no pens, pencils, lamps, flower pots, *nothing*. Nothing a suicidal teenager could use for suicide. It was an approach to interior décor I'd seen in films about crazy people who drool, pull their hair out, and eat their own tongues. *Great*. This was a place for nutjobs. My parents had concluded I was nuts. So nuts that they didn't feel comfortable driving me to the nut house themselves. Like maybe I would take control of the steering wheel and steer us into oncoming traffic.

"How are you feeling?" nurse Lorine asked. *Lorine*. Nice woman. Strong woman. Someone you could trust if she weren't in this place.

"Fine," I said.

"Are you hungry, thirsty?"

"No."

"Have you taken anything you shouldn't have today? Alcohol, drugs, pills, glue?"

Glue? Jesus. "No."

"Well, you're in good hands here. We understand what you're going through. Everything's going to be just fine."

If I didn't know what I was going through, how could she? Maybe this was where they kept the instruction manuals for troubled teens with authority problems who fake suicides with steak knives. Maybe she'd thumb through it, find my make and model, run some diagnostics, and fix stuff.

"You lie down for a few minutes. I need to fill out some paperwork to get you admitted, and then I'm going to come back to take some blood tests, sugar."

Admitted. A word you should never trust under any circumstances.

I stalked the room, peering out the small, unbreakable

window to see if there were any more like her and any more like me. This seemed like the sort of place where they harvested psycho teenagers. I wanted to see whether they had nice hair and good tans like me. Or if they looked wild and sunken, their eyes on a lifelong journey to the back of their skulls.

A steak knife? Why did I do that? If I'd just pouted and sulked my father probably would've let me off and I would've drunk wine coolers with that girl with the breasts.

Damn.

Tears spoiled the tough-as-nails, you-can't-crack-me image I had been planning. Fifteen minutes later, the nurse returned. She sat next to me on the gymnast pad, placed a reassuring hand on my thigh, and told me that she needed to take some blood tests.

"Nope," I said.

"I know, I know, no one likes doing this. However —"

"Nope."

"Troy, we have to —"

"Fuck off," I barked, more sad than angry. In a place like this, I was willing to bet cussing at adults was expected.

She sighed and looked at me with pity — patient, adult pity. She slapped both of her knees and smiled as if this happened all the time, as if I wasn't the first. She'd eventually get my blood like the rest.

"Okay, I'll come back in a few minutes to see if you're feeling better," she said.

About a half hour later, she returned to yet another cuss word. I couldn't believe I was here. Normal me. Well-adjusted me. In a rubber room.

She came back. I cussed. She left.

This went on for nearly an hour. Finally, she said, "You know, the longer you keep this up, the harder it's going to be. And the longer you'll be here. And honey, if you don't let me do it this time, then I have to call in some big men who are gonna tie you down, and we'll take your blood anyway. They're a lot less patient than I am."

I let her pull blood from my arm. I called her a bitch under my breath. It didn't faze her.

She pulled more blood silently and patiently. How many gallons did they need? Apparently you can't tell crazy from just one. A billowing wet cloud of my craziness flowed up into the plastic syringe.

"There, that's it," she said. "All finished. That wasn't so bad, was it?"

"Whatever," I muttered. She needed to know I wasn't to be fucked with. But she had kindness in her eyes. I withered into a sulk.

"You think you're ready to get out of this room and get a room of your own?" she asked.

"Whatever. Sure."

She led me down the hall. We passed a large window in the hallway. On the other side sat eight or so teenagers — rough, haggard, normal, blond, black, happy, sad, emotionless teenagers. They were watching TV, twisting their fingers through their hair — normal teenager stuff, except behind a large pane of glass in Charter Hospital where they could be monitored.

The nurse opened a door to the left. "Here you go," she said. "In a few days you'll get a roommate. But for now, this is all yours — your own bachelor pad. In the bathroom you'll find some toiletries — toothpaste, toothbrush, soap, deodorant. If you need anything else, just pick up this phone and hit 'operator.'"

Just like a hotel. Sooner or later I'd dial "operator" and order some room service. Eggs, bacon, blueberry muffins, a couple liters of Coke. That would get a laugh.

"Your mother is bringing down some more clothes and some of your personal stuff in just a while," the nurse said. "I'll be back in a few minutes, and we'll show you around and introduce you to everyone."

Outside this room lay the world. My friends were out there, miles away, eating lunch in the cafeteria, talking about girls, and making stupid jokes.

I lay down on the bed. The events that led me here made little sense. I pictured standing at the end of our hallway at home. My mother was in her bed, sobbing, wiping the tears with one tissue after another. I stood there yelling, "I hate you! I fucking hate you! You've ruined my life! I fucking *hate* you!"

My first roommate was a large, mushy guy with tight, curly black hair. His face reminded me of olives.

"You know any party tricks?" he asked one night after we'd been ordered to our rooms to sleep.

"I dunno," I replied. "Not really."

"I can fart for six minutes straight," he announced, proudly. "That's my record."

Farting was still a marketable skill in my social circles.

Anyone who could do it at will was a minor celebrity. Anyone who timed himself doing it for six full minutes belonged in a mental ward.

"Bullshit," I said. "Let's hear it."

"Okay, okay," he said, more excited than a person should be about the prospect of nonstop flatulence. He got on all fours in bed, his ass moving back and forth in partial darkness. After about thirty seconds, I said, "Aw, you're a liar — you can't do it." I was genuinely disappointed.

"No, wait, lemme get warmed up," he said, laughing. And then, sure enough, he started farting — a sound for when the air sucked inside his ass, and a sound when his ass exhaled.

I laughed uncontrollably. A single burst of flatulence was punch line enough in my world. That this strange, vaguely psychotic teenager could fart in symphony was beyond hilarious. In the absence of more normal social skills, this kid had learned to use his anus to bond with people like me.

After about three minutes the mood in the room — to say nothing of the smell — changed. "What're you gay, dude?" I snipped. "You gotta be gay. That's the only kind of ass I know that could do that." Insulted, he stopped.

Two days later, he was gone. Apparently his teenage psyche and prolific posterior were deemed suitable for life in the outside world.

After I had been in Charter for three days, my parents came to visit. The head doctor — a grayish man with caterpillar eyebrows and dead eyes — called me into the office and briefed me on the proceedings. This apparently was where I started the reconciliation process — where we dug beneath the steak knife, past the late-night doggie-door shimmies, the Herculean truancy, and discovered the decayed, withering root that was feeding bad lifeblood into me.

"Troy, your parents are here," he said. "They want to talk to you."

"I don't have anything to say to them," I said.

"I realize you're angry at them for putting you in here. You don't think you belong here, right?"

"I *know* I don't."

"Okay, well, this is how you get out of here. Do you think you should let them know how angry you are, why you're angry? You can say anything you want in here. You can't say anything wrong, and no one's going to lecture you."

I reiterated my intention of silence.

My mother was crying when she and my father entered the room. For the first ten years of my life, the sight of her crying drove me to inconsolable sadness. I usually hugged her and attacked whoever inspired her tears. By the time I was eleven, however, this crying had become suspect. She used it too often. I began to feel manipulated by the crying. I began to hate it.

I looked at my parents, rolled my eyes, and picked a wall to stare at.

"Okay — Cathie, Rich, Troy — we're here today to try to understand what has made Troy angry. His anger is real, and, Cathie and Rich, we've spoken. I know you respect that. Troy, can you tell us *why you're angry?*"

Silence. My parents blathered for fifteen minutes

about how much they loved me and how much they wished I'd talk to them.

More silence.

Finally they left. My mother hugged me, my body slack, my arms at my side. *You're dead to me.* These visitations continued every few days for the next month.

One of my closest pals in the ward was Cheryl, a fifteen-year-old Indian girl with a huge scar that cut her face almost exactly in half.

"My stepfather cut me," she said, and that was that. I didn't know if she was lying or "transferring her anger" — a phrase I learned during our first group therapy session. Either way, I didn't want to hear more.

Cheryl was a wake-up call. My mother hadn't cut me. She hadn't hit me with a hot waffle iron in a drunken fit. She was just gay, which made me feel abnormal. She had become something I wanted to hide, to tuck away in a room and visit when I needed love. My scars were internal.

During group therapy, Cheryl taught me how to blow spit bubbles. Although I had appreciated the talents of my departed roommate, forming a bubble out of spit and blowing it onto an unsuspecting victim six feet away proved much more useful.

The one person onto whom I never blew one was Delicia — a large black girl whose muscle mass complemented her permanent scowl. "Her name is Latin for 'delight,'" our group counselor explained. Minutes later Delicia threw a desk across the room and threatened to fight us all.

She growled like a dog that had just realized it was about to be neutered.

When an even larger black orderly came in to subdue her, "Delight" yelled that he was a pawn of the white man — "Just another nigger on the payroll!" The nigger on the payroll wrestled her down. Half our therapy sessions ended with a pile of people on top of Delicia.

Delicia's counterpoint was Tom, a tall, hulking boy with a buzz cut. Had he not shown the ability to walk and chew food, you might have concluded that he was dead. Doctors had stuffed him with enough antidepressants to make him look like a toy doll built to appear unimpressed. ("Pull the doll's string, and watch it ignore you!")

"Hey, I'm Troy," I said when first encountering him in group.

His neck rotated with alarming, fluid slowness. "Tom," he said. His voice sounded as though he'd gone through puberty three, maybe four times. His hand was muscular but uncommitted. I shook our hands up and down in salutation. When I released his hand, it fell back into his lap, and he slowly turned back toward the group leader.

That was the first and last time we spoke. But every day I watched him, waiting for this massive boy to snap back to life and destroy something. For someone who seemed capable of an enormous physical outburst — possibly knocking out four or five orderlies in a psychotic rage — he was a marvel of how little a human body could move and still be considered an animate object. He, too, disappeared one day. His parents' health insurance no doubt expired.

The staff at Charter regimented our days. Three square meals in a cafeteria just like the one at high school. Large women made of sorrow and cellulite wore hairnets and scooped food, the flabby undersides of their arms nearly drooping into the potatoes. The meals were healthier, however: apples instead of french fries, juice dispensers where the soda machines would have been. One of the program's theories was that foods high in fat and sugar caused craziness. Apparently celery can prevent suicide.

In the misguided belief that one kind of crazy neutralized another, I had decided in group therapy that the best approach to my recovery was through a series of smarmy, bitter comments.

"Troy, why are you in here, do you think?" one group leader asked.

"Because my parents are dickheads," I replied.

"Why are they dickheads?"

"I would be, too, if I woke up one day and realized I was a total asshole."

The other patients snickered. I was the class clown just as I'd always been in the outside world. Ignoring my life with unfunny humor made me feel normal. It was my rudimentary power play.

I didn't mention I was completely incapable of dealing with a gay parent, that the shame was waging a bloody feud with my sense of self-importance. I didn't mention that I resented my mother for feeling stuck with her. That

I had wanted to defect to my father's house just as my sister had. I wanted the postcard family. Which, I knew, meant abandoning her — and I loved her terribly. Everyone in her life had deserted her — either by death or by simply walking away. I couldn't bring myself to be the last deserter, the one who finally broke her.

So I stayed and made her miserable right up until I pointed a steak knife at my gut, then found myself here with kids who couldn't sleep at night because they never knew if an adult with flammable breath would crawl in bed with them.

My problem felt small and trite by comparison, which pissed me off even more. Having divorced parents and a mom who slept with other women sure felt like a real fucking problem. The other kids at Charter were denying me the right to hold on to my anger and pull it out every time I was caught breaking laws.

The craft room was the nexus of life at Charter. Some art fag in mental health had decided that painting and ceramics could lead to psychological breakthroughs. We could access our inner sane person through the proper use of the color spectrum. From what I could tell, it just led to bad art.

My creative genius manifested as a dinosaur soap dispenser. I poured various clay mixtures into a mold and then a trained professional put it into a kiln. My dinosaur emerged looking like a psychedelic version of Dino from *The Flintstones*. I poured soap in its belly and shoved a pump down its throat. I didn't feel any saner for the experience, but a small feeling of pride warmed inside me. Destruction had been routine — my sister's dolls, jazz records, house windows — but creating something was a new experience.

After the third parent–head shrink conference, my doctor began to tell me repeatedly that I didn't belong in Charter. He promised to send me home if I spoke to my parents just once. But I was pretty fascinated by this place and had more silence to air, so I stayed.

One night, I attempted to take real drugs for the first time. Not the sort that are measured in milligrams, come in a paper cup, and are administered by a certified professional. I attempted to take the fun kind — the kind that are measured by hits and are administered by the nearest delinquent with bad personal hygiene.

My sherpas into the world of street pharmacology were Jeremy and Vince, two kids who shared a deep and abiding love of heavy metal music, who had inexplicably been assigned to be roommates. Maybe Charter figured they'd start a band. Maybe some Berkeley doctor had concluded power chords were the new Paxil.

Jeremy was a gangly white kid with long, stringy hair that had been dyed so many times that the follicles were nearly translucent. He never finished a conversation without throwing the universal hand sign for devil horns. Charter reportedly admitted him after he sacrificed a black cat in the middle of summer.

"Halloween's for amateurs," he told us. "Any dork who owns a Motley Crüe album can skin a cat. To do it right, you've got to really *know* evil."

No one believed the cat story. To which his response was, "Fine. Then don't call me when you can't find Fluffy."

Vince had a rippling upper body he'd cultivated with numerous bench presses. His skinny legs, however, suggested he didn't have a great sense of proportion. He looked like a rooster on 'roids. He owned an impressive collection of black T-shirts that appeared to have been dipped in municipal waste and left outside to dry. He didn't talk much. Cheryl and I concluded that he really liked Wham! and had a collection of ceramic ponies displayed on his dresser at home.

One day after group, I visited their room to find them lying on their beds, laughing hysterically. Jeremy's face was purple, and saliva percolated at the corners of his mouth. He was holding the sides of his head with both hands, as if trying to make sure nothing escaped.

"Troy, Troy, Troy!" Vince said mid-laugh. "You gotta tell me — do you see a fairy up in that corner?" He pointed to the empty corner of the room where the wall met the ceiling.

"Uhhhhhhh . . . are you fucking serious?" I asked. Maybe the Charter staff had seriously goofed and given them way too many meds. Or maybe this was it. Maybe I was walking into the exact moment when people go from mildly disturbed to totally, bat-shit crazy.

He and Jeremy continued laughing, silently deciding whether to let me in on their hilarious secret.

"I swear, I just saw a fairy . . . it was pink . . . the little wings . . . and *right fucking there*," Jeremy stammered. "It had a wand . . . Fuck! That was *crazy*."

"Shhhhhhhhhh." Vince laughed, his finger to his lips. "We took some acid."

"What? How?" I asked.

"It's liquid," Vince clarified. "We smuggled some in our toothpaste. It's awesome."

"Fucking *awesome*," Jeremy agreed.

"Can I try some?" I asked without hesitating. I'd never done real drugs before. But then again, I'd never been in a loony bin before, either. Life seemed ripe, and opportunity was knocking.

"Sure, man. Not sure if there's any left — squeeze some of the Crest onto your finger."

Jeremy directed me into the bathroom, where I grabbed the toothpaste. I took off the cap and hesitated. I'd heard horror stories about what LSD did to people. Teenagers jumped off roofs and cut their faces off with glass shards. But then I heard Jeremy laugh in the other room — a contagious, full-body seizure of happiness — and realized maybe I'd been deceived. Maybe parents told you drugs were bad so they could keep them for themselves. Plus, seeing invisible fairies sounded a lot like being a child again. If there was anything I really wanted at this point in my life, it was to feel like a kid again, to remember what it was like to have invisible friends and feel like that was completely normal.

I squeezed a glob of Crest onto my forefinger. *Last chance to back out*, I thought. I put it in my mouth. Tasted like toothpaste. For some reason, I hadn't expected that.

"Did you take it?" Vince asked when I emerged from the bathroom.

"Yep," I said, heart racing.

"It'll take about a half hour before you feel anything,"

said Jeremy, who was obviously an expert in the ways of LSD.

"Just hang out until we have to go to dinner," Vince said.

Jeremy talked more about the fairy. He taught Vince a trick his older brother had taught him — wave your hands in front of your face and you see trails. Hands like shooting stars.

Every five minutes or so, one of them asked, "Feel anything yet?"

"No."

Five more minutes.

"Yet?"

"No."

"How 'bout now?"

"I think I feel something," I lied. Part of me wanted to laugh and see fairies. Another part of me was scared shitless.

At dinner, Jeremy and Vince's carrots were apparently doing stand-up comedy. The two boys poked their mashed potatoes, making spud sculptures à la *Close Encounters of the Third Kind*. They did everything to their food except eat it.

I kept waiting for my carrots to dance. I pretended to shoo a fly away from my plate, watching for trails behind my hands.

Nothing.

The mental health counselors apparently knew what makes carrots endlessly fascinating. Lorine came over with a large orderly and said, "Jeremy, Vince, come with me."

They were still laughing as the nurses led them out of the cafeteria.

I felt thankful that I wasn't getting busted. I imagined my parents' faces when the head counselor told them, "Well, Troy has shown some signs of progress, but he did take acid and had a hallucination involving fairies and dancing carrots."

Unfortunately, my first attempt to do drugs only ended up making potatoes taste like Crest.

After we'd all been sent to our rooms for the night, I took all of the clothes out of my drawer and piled them on my bed in the form of a human body.

"That's never gonna work. You're gonna get busted," said my new roommate. He couldn't fart on command, and had no other impressive skills. I concluded he was sent to Charter for being clinically boring. "What do I tell them when they come looking for you?" he whined.

"Just tell 'em you were asleep and don't know," I snapped.

A nurse sat beyond the glass door at the end of the hallway. She was busy with paperwork, probably trying to explain how two metal heads got their hands on LSD. I darted into the hallway and ran two rooms down, opening the door to see the outline of Lana's body.

Initially, my advances hadn't impressed Lana. Her blond hair and sleepy blue eyes suggested she was only truly comfortable in her own skin if she were in bed, wearing a nightie. Her lips were full, like a whole vagina on her face.

We had planned this tryst for a few days. Her roommate had been dispatched into the real world. Lana had the room to herself until another San Diego teen lost it and moved in.

"Is this where they keep the psycho girls?" I said in a stage whisper.

"Shut up — close the door!" she said, propping herself up in bed.

Lana came from a very wealthy family of solid breeding. I came from a less opulent strand of DNA. I think she finally caved because she realized that necking with me would displease her parents immensely — like an heiress eloping with a bike messenger. All of us were looking for ways to get back at our parents for putting us in this place.

For the next twenty minutes, we assaulted each other with our lips. The sort of empty, melodramatic kissing that makes movie stars millions of dollars. My hand slid up her shirt, but she blocked it. I tried to slip off her cotton shorts.

"You should go," she said.

"Sorry — sorry. Can I just lie next to you?" I pleaded.

She sighed and allowed it, and I rested my head directly atop her fifteen-year-old breasts without the least bit of subtlety. It was comforting, nearly maternal.

Five minutes later we heard the bellowing voice of the large female nurse who patrolled the ward on weeknights. I leapt from the bed, darted into the hallway, and flew back to my room. The lights were on, the sheets pulled back from my pile of clothes that was supposed to resemble a human body. The nurse appeared at the door. "Mr. Johnson, come with me."

Had everything gone right, the newspaper headline the next morning would have read, "Boy on LSD Impregnates Beauty Queen in Mental Ward." Instead, my journal entry read, "Failed at drugs, can't even get laid by crazy girls." I lost outside privileges for three days for my failures.

In those three days, my anger at my parents cooled. The loony bin was costing them $900 a day, so at least I was punching them in their pocketbooks. But they hadn't yet said "uncle," and I was starting to think they might just leave me there.

At my next meeting with the head shrink, I announced that I would talk to them. Really, I wasn't mad at my father. He was a neutered, third-party parent who lived in another house. All of my anger directed itself at my mother. Having a gay parent wasn't like having a Mohawk or a piercing. You can't just pull it out of your face and let the hole close up. Having a gay parent was beyond my control. It had been forced on me, and I couldn't sculpt it in a way that made it cool.

"Rich, Cathie — Troy is ready to start making some headway," he said. "And, honestly, I think one productive session and Troy should be ready to go home."

Obviously this man wanted to get rid of me. My parents thought I might be seriously troubled, but this man rightly saw me as just another pubescent teen who egged on desk-throwing psychos and tried to hump his trust-fund patients.

My parents didn't question his haste. They wanted to save my life, not get rid of their loud, angry teenage problem. By this time — considerably poorer — they also knew I had used family cutlery just to get attention.

In that one productive session, we talked about a lot of

things — everything except my huge problem with having a lesbian for a mom. For years, I had pretended it wasn't that big of a deal, so everyone thought my problem lay elsewhere — drugs, depression, my truant pubic hair.

We hugged, we cried, and a day later I was released.

Besides a dramatically improved emotional state — if only by seeing what truly twisted teenagers were like — the only thing I took with me from the experience at Charter was the psychedelic dinosaur soap dispenser.

Chapter

13

Home o' Phobia

AFTER I WAS RELEASED from Charter Hospital, I wasn't allowed to return to high school until the following school year, so Dad required that I get a job. He hoped it would give me a taste of the real world — the name tag–wearing service industry world to which his prodigal son seemed destined.

My father knew that a lack of structure in my life would eventually lead to my name being spoken by an evening news anchor using his "serious face." *(I've been practicing all week, boss. Check it out — does this say "double homicide" or what?)*

My first paying gig — as a towel boy at the car wash — indeed prepared me for the real world. My boss, an Italian man in his thirties who moved his neck like an aroused rooster, gave me advice on romance.

"Have you ever come on a woman's face? You're not

a real man until you jizz all over her hair." He placed his hands about six inches in front of his crotch — an exaggerated visual, I'm sure — arched his back, and swung his hips as if he were urinating his name in snow.

Our job was to huddle and wait for cars to emerge from the automatic wash. My Mexican coworkers sized up each female customer and taught me how to talk about them in Spanish. To this day, I can walk into any Tijuana brothel and capably order a woman with "tits like mountains and the ass of an elephant."

California law prohibited me from driving at age fifteen, so my father enlisted my grandmother as my chauffeur. She drove one of those long sedans marketed solely to those who may die very soon. Her Granny Sedan was the color of baby diarrhea and smelled like old people. The real problem, though, was that Grandma Dorothy was a loon. Not crazy as in "she occasionally puts peanut butter on her eggs." Crazy as in, before she died she told me that Saddam Hussein was running a covert operation involving hospice workers.

"She's one of them," she said, pointing to the nice, rotund woman who was helping Grandma die with dignity.

Grandma also compulsively clipped. If she saw an inspirational quote in one of her Christian magazines — "Accept God Now or Die in a Skiing Accident Tomorrow," for instance — she clipped it out and wrote "Send to Troy" on it. Then she'd file it away in one of the hundreds of empty Kleenex boxes she used as tiny filing cabinets.

Sometimes she actually mailed those clippings. Mostly she just piled them all over the place until my father and I had to perform an intervention. We entered her apartment with an econo-pack of garbage bags and stuffed every last one with assorted crap — which Grandma had stacked everywhere, save for tiny pathways to the bathroom, kitchen, bedroom, front door, and her favorite chair.

Grandma loved her crap. Crap has never felt such love. So our crap removal expeditions crushed the poor woman's soul. In one of the adventures, I was disposing of approximately half — *half* — of the four thousand plastic grocery bags she had stockpiled in her pantry for the Great Plastic Bag Shortage to come.

"Ohhhhh, noooooooo," she whined. "Troy, you never know when you'll need a plastic bag."

"Grandma, if you ever find yourself in need of *two thousand* plastic bags, I will get them for you."

"Oh, okay, fine," she said. "When you're done with that, you can toss my bed. Unscrew the toilet and take it with you, too." Then she put her hand over her heart and hyperventilated in her favorite chair.

Yet, for some reason, Grandma and I got along. It was the magnetism of the mutually crazy, I guess. After alienating pretty much everyone else in the family, she needed an ally. And I was the nice gullible child who looked exactly like my father. She took me for her own.

For the first few days she drove me to work, everything went smoothly. We chatted about how I was going to straighten out my life. I told her all about Charter — the desk-thrower, the dinosaur pump, the "invaluable growth."

She told me that God was the only way back for me. Jesus and I were seeing other people at the time, so I wasn't so sure. Especially because getting back together with Jesus meant hanging with people who thought my mom was a sin-pig, rooting her snout in whatever trough of vice she could find. And no one was allowed to hate my mother — no one but me.

On the third day of driving me to work, Grandma told me another thing about God. He had bent her ear and told her to tell me that my mother was — and I quote — "A DIRTY, FILTHY LESBIAN WHO IS GOING STRAIGHT TO HELL! A MONSTROSITY! AGAINST GOD'S WILL! SHE'LL MEET SATAN ALONG WITH ALL THE MURDERERS AND PROSTITUTES AND THAT SLUT YOUR FATHER MARRIED!"

She was shrieking. Her old, ashen face hadn't flushed with such Technicolor rage since the 1950s. Little pieces of food even flew from her mouth with each new breath of invective. *Why don't old people ever fully swallow their food?* I thought.

"YOU'RE NOT SICK! SHE IS! SHE MADE YOU THIS WAY, PUT YOU IN THAT CRAZY BIN BE-CAUSE YOU WERE SICK FROM TRYING TO PUT UP WITH HER SICK, SICK LIFESTYLE!"

While I wanted to agree — it *was* Mom's fault! — Grandma's rage was disorienting, frightening. If you want to meet the most bigoted people in the world, don't go to a redneck country bar. Go lawn bowling.

"IT HAPPENED AT SODOM! GAY PEOPLE RAPED AN ENTIRE VILLAGE OF CHRISTIANS! THEY'RE THE DEVIL'S WORK!"

While I folded my arms and hummed the *CHiPs* theme song, she impressively hollered for the entire ten-minute drive.

When we finally reached the car wash, I opened the door and got out. "Grandma, you may be right about my mother going to hell," I told her, "but you're a fucking bitch." It wasn't a phenomenal comeback — definitely not a zinger — but it felt good. I was fully okay with extending my "therapeutic potty mouth" practices to grandmas. Especially ones who smelled old and gave ten-minute monologues about my mother's stain on Planet Christian Earth.

As you might expect, Grandma and I didn't speak for a while. I'm sure her apartment overflowed with magazine clippings such as "How to Exorcise Satan from Your Grandchildren."

If it had just been Pat Robertson and old war generals telling me that my mother was a tenth-class citizen for being gay, I could handle it. But my own family often reminded me that I was living with *one of them.*

My dad was the most understanding about Mom being gay. He never called her a dyke or suggested that I move in with him because a boy needs a "real" family. In fact, he urged me to accept my mother for who she was. Trouble was, he didn't — or, rather, couldn't.

In the first few years after Mom came out, Dad always prefaced social gatherings with a plea: "Hey, buddy, don't mention anything about your mom being gay in front of these people. I'm kind of embarrassed about it."

Dad knew when he was being superficial and small. He was very up front about it, admitted it was more about his own issues. Granted, the ex-husband of a woman who blossoms into a lesbian has a special circumstance. Maybe he made her lose faith in the penis.

My dad taught me it was okay to be embarrassed by Mom.

Then there's my uncle — a funny, intelligent man liked by everyone. Stick him in a room with a bunch of gays, though, and you'd think he was an alcoholic tax accountant with a huge social phobia and no access to liquor. Still, I don't blame him. He hails from the last generation taught that homos are cannibals. He probably called my grandfather a racist when the latter watched the Ali-Frazier fight and said, "Man, I love seeing two monkeys beat the hell out of each other — hand me the chips." My uncle was born in the generation that knew black people. But by the time gays made their big entrance in 1969, my uncle had already grown up, and most grown-ups are tired of growing.

Every time a conversation turned to my mother, he said a few kind words about her before adding, "Man, I really like your mom, but that whole lesbian thing — I just don't get it." His face would scrunch up as if he'd mistaken a glass of battery acid for a margarita. "She still . . . y'know?" asked, making the universal hand sign for scissors and bumping them together.

I laughed and then told my own lesbian jokes. These jokes represented the first real step in coming to terms with her sexuality. If you can laugh at it, you can deal with it. My uncle taught me that it was okay to make jokes on Mom's account.

My step-grandmother was equally dismissive. Her face soured whenever Mom's name came up. She once spent an entire night at a pizza joint telling the whole family how disgusting it was that my mother was a lesbian. I sat at the end of the table, gnawing on my crust.

The list goes on — aunts, uncles, in-laws, step-people. No family member crusaded in defense of my mother. No one dissented during these fun little bash sessions. Besides the elderly in my family — who had reached the *fuck it, I'll say what I please* portion of their time on earth — no one was blatantly cruel about it. But all of them implicitly — and, at times, explicitly — wrote her off and assigned the pervert clause to her name.

This was my family — otherwise good people I loved and respected — whom I was told would teach me good from bad. Seeing as how it takes a child a few years to learn how to say, "Grandpa, that's quite small of you, and quite frankly, homophobic," I was very susceptible to group-think.

Chapter

14

Freaks Everywhere

MY MOTHER TRIED TO FACILITATE my transition from mortified son of a lesbian to simply son of a lesbian. Eventually, she hoped I'd become proud son of a lesbian — "What're you looking at?"

I, on the other hand, was perfectly fine with the big gay elephant in our living room. I acknowledged it daily, kicked its hard, pudgy shins and went about my business.

"Hey, sport," she said one day. "Got a minute?"

Uh-oh. Anytime a parent begins with "got a minute," it means twenty minutes for a lecture about how you're too old to be doing whatever juvenile behavior you're thoroughly enjoying.

"Listen, I know you still aren't really okay with the fact that I've chosen to date women," she said.

"Yeah, kinda. I mean, it's your business, not mine," I lied.

"Well, it affects you. I know it's gotta be tough," she said. "Believe me, it was tough on me for a while. You probably feel like you're the only kid on the planet with a gay parent, right?"

"I haven't met any yet — well, besides Tattle Dyke's daughters. And they sucked."

Logic told me there were other kids with gay parents, but I figured that they also kicked the gay elephant. They, like me, were waiting for the moment at the breakfast table when their parent announced, "Mmm, I love bacon. By the way, I'm not gay anymore. Sorry to put you through that. Tell you what, to make up for it, why don't we go buy you a truck? I know you're only twelve, but in four years you'll be so glad to have it."

"Here, take a look at this," my mother said, handing me a pamphlet. On the front it said, "COLAGE." It had a photo of kids of all shapes and ethnicities — all the colors of Benetton. They exuded an unnatural happiness that said, *Every other aspect of my life completely and utterly sucks. I'd actually kill myself if it weren't for this moment. I'm a brochure model now, which fills me with immense, immeasurable happiness.*

"What's this?"

"It's an organization called COLAGE. Well, 'organization' isn't really the right word. It's just a bunch of normal kids like you with parents like me."

Anything that had to "organize" filled me with suspicion. My one experience with an organization — the

Christian Church — hadn't worked out so well. If you need to form a support group to keep an idea going, your idea isn't working.

"It stands for Children of Lesbians and Gays Everywhere," she said.

The goal of this COLAGE was to "engage, connect, and empower people to make the world a better place for children of lesbian, gay, bisexual, and/or transgender parents and families."

Great. Just fucking great. Not only was it trying enough to have a gay parent, but now that gay parent wanted to send me to an Alternative After-School Special Program. Plus, if these COLAGE kids actually were accepting of their gay parents, then I definitely wanted no part of them. I didn't want any acceptance tainting my pure strain of intolerance.

I imagined a group of us sitting around. Someone would have a bar through her nose and facial tattoos. Organizers would have seeded the group with a few undercover actors, kids without gay parents acting like they had gay parents and it was the greatest thing that had ever happened to them — better than masturbation or Led Zeppelin!

Unable to stay silent for more than ten seconds, I'd blurt out, "So mine's a dyke — what's yours?"

A counselor would interrupt, "Troy, you mean *lesbian*, right?" Then the counselor would make a bad joke. "Gay women only retain water *once* a month . . . *ha ha ha*."

"Yeah, right, so mine's a *lesbian*, and holy god is it embarrassing. How do we switch 'er back?"

I told my mom how I felt about COLAGE: "No thanks, Mom. Y'know, I already have tennis and surfing. I barely have time for my own friends."

"Really?" she said, giving me the understanding yet disappointed look.

"Yeah," I said, cutting to the chase. "Please don't make me."

"No no no, of course not," she said. "You don't have to do anything you don't want to. But I would love it if . . . Maybe if you have some free time some day . . . Maybe just check it out. . . . Who knows, you might even make some friends. I think it'd be really good for you."

And there it was. The clincher. Anytime a parent says, "It would be really good for you," it means that you will want to throw yourself in front of a moving vehicle if you ever participate in said activity.

"I'll think about it," I lied. "But I don't think so."

Going to a meeting of COLAGE group would count as an official recognition of my gay mom. Mom and Gay Mom were still two separate people in my head, like Dr. Jekyll and Mrs. Hyde. Gay Mom was an undesirable alter ego whom I was willing to ignore as a gesture of goodwill to the mom I loved.

In my head, COLAGE was part of my mother's heterosexual extraction conspiracy. Gay Mom was trying to take me away from all my friends with straight parents. What next, playing in some sort of kids of queers tennis league? Would we start inviting other gay families over for dinner to talk about intra-family dynamics? Did COLAGE have its own school system?

No matter how gay Mom was, she would not make me include more gay in my life. Her sexuality was only part of my life in the same way that laundry or washing the dishes were. I dealt with it only when not dealing with it resulted in extraordinary chaos and suffering.

Chapter

15

The Man of My Dreams

I WAS LISTENING TO MOTLEY CRÜE'S new album in my bedroom, thinking about growing out my hair and wearing black eye makeup. I was beginning to realize that Kim and her friend Crystal had been on to something. Between songs, I heard my mother talking to someone in the living room.

The lesbo parade, I thought.

But then I heard it. The person responding to her spoke in a deep, resonant voice, like the muted horn of a cruise ship. I slunk down the hallway to eavesdrop. The voice spoke again. It said something casual — about a different town where it had spent time. My mother asked the voice more questions. Cruise Ship answered with ease, laughed a little.

Was it — *it can't be* — yes! It was a *man*! And he wasn't here to fix our washing machine. This was a social call. I nearly crapped myself.

I marched into the living room for confirmation. My mother sat on the couch, and Cruise Ship sat in the adjacent chair. *Oh my god, they were drinking wine!* And out of the same tiny pottery cups that my mother and Tattle Dyke used when they were relaxing with the help of Ernest & Julio Gallo.

Play it cool. Don't beg.

"Hey there," Cruise Ship said. He looked like a firefighter who'd lost his sight in a smoke-related incident and spent his disability money on fast food. He was perfect.

"Hello," I said, deciding not to warn him how much dog hair was probably stuck to the butt of his pants. "Who are you?"

He laughed. He probably thought I was the protective son still reeling from my parents' divorce and shielding her from inferior suitors.

I will give you a thousand dollars to date my mother, I thought. *I don't have the thousand dollars right now, but if you date my mother I swear within one week's time I will knock off a liquor store and give it to you as a dowry. And then I will humbly serve you, great Muted Horn of Cruise Ship Man.*

"This," my mother chuckled, "is my son, Troy. Troy, this is Bob, a friend from work."

Get up from your chair right now, wipe off the dog hair, walk over and plant a big, passionate movie kiss on her. Now. You have no idea, Cruise Ship, what I have been through.

"Nice to meet you," I said, straightening out my posture and smiling in a way that said, *This is a happy house — a house of joy! You will not regret coming to live here.* "Can I get you guys anything? More wine?"

My mother's eyes eyebrows raised; she smiled. I wasn't

the most attentive, obedient child. But she had never brought home a *man*! To drink from the social ceramic cups! If there was one way to turn me into a dutiful child, this was it.

Sure, I always hoped Mom would go hetero again, but that hope I placed next to "grope Farah Fawcett" on my list of wishes that would never happen. My mother had spent months in therapy trying to figure out how to tell her family that she was gay. When we found out, it tore the family apart. She lost friends. Why would a woman put herself through all that unless she was absolutely sure that she really, *really* didn't dig dudes?

Children often ruin "the moment." I'd seen it on TV. So I said a polite good-bye and left the room so they could dedicate their undying eternal love to each other. I turned the corner of the hallway and pressed my back against the wall, listening to their entire conversation. He grew up in Cincinnati, liked the weather in San Diego, and, no thanks, he didn't want another glass of wine.

Shit.

I thought about puncturing his car tires. Then I would demand to fix them. "No, you're a house guest, and this happened on our property," I'd say. "You guys just talk some more, and I'll have it done in a jiffy." I would then take an hour to fix each tire.

He didn't stay long. After about fifteen minutes, he said it was late and that he should go. I listened to him leave, wondering if you could actually hear two people embrace. There was no kissing sound. As soon as the door shut, I turned the corner.

"Who was that?"

Mom laughed at my instantaneous curiosity.

"That's just Bob, a friend from work. We went out to dinner."

"Was it a *date*?" I asked.

"I don't know if I'd call it that, but you never know," she said with a shrug and a smile.

"What do you mean you never *know*? How did it go? Do you *like* him?"

"You'd like that, wouldn't you?" she asked. She wasn't offended. She knew I was openly campaigning for more men in her life. Going through the process of a "new family" wasn't very appealing, but I wanted to plug all the available holes in my mother's social life with men. Doing so, I figured, blocked women — kind of like the game Connect Four, but with people instead of plastic checkers.

"He's a nice man," she said, "but it wasn't really a date."

"Are you going to see him again?"

"We'll see," she said with finality. "We'll see."

I asked about Bob regularly for the next three months. He was my personal savior, my avatar. He had no idea what hope he had cast into my life. It was like a bearded hippie walked across a shallow puddle and I was the nutjob who thought he saw Jesus.

"Have you seen Bob again?" — "What kind of car does he drive? A Mercedes? Mom, he's rich!" — "Hey, why don't you invite Bob to the Padres game? He can have my ticket. I'm kinda over baseball, anyway." — "Maybe you should call him. Guys like it when you call them."

Relentless.

Finally, after I asked if she and Bob ever had lunch together in the work cafeteria, my mother closed the discussion. "It was one dinner, three months ago. It was nothing." Seeing the defeated look in my face, she added, "Look, I know how you feel. And I'm open to being with a man again. You never know. I fall in love with the person, whether it's a man or a woman. We'll just have to wait and see. It may just be me and you for a while."

I have since learned that only lesbians, it seems, say that they fall in love with a person regardless of gender.

"That's okay," I said. I understood. More than a few preteen girls had shunned me. I knew what it was like to be unwanted. "His loss."

Mom smiled, tousled my hair.

I did want her to be happy. I wanted her to find true romance. I just wanted to have a say in who she found it with. Were there any portly teachers at school who seemed like their wives had left them? I could invent some scholastic emergency that could only be solved by a home visit. When they arrived, I would call out my mother and crack open a bottle of wine.

And this time, I'd definitely slash the tires. And set the car on fire.

Chapter

16

Not in My House, Lady

"WHEN YOU HAVE CHILDREN, YOU'RE GROUNDED."

A friend's mother once told me this. To make sure their offspring don't butter toast with denture cream or experiment with fire and the family cat, parents forgo a social life. No more swing-dancing lessons, no more art gallery galas. Grab a glass of milk, strap on some ammo, and guard the door.

My mom was grounded more than most.

By the time I was sixteen, she had been out of the closet for six years. Half a dozen years of living with a gay parent, and I was still alive. Okay, a dramatic interlude with a steak knife had led to a month in a mental hospital, and I was regularly ditching high school, but no truly catastrophic psychiatric fallout had resulted from cohabitating with a homo.

My mother had been with her partner, Louise, for

two years. Louise was a recovering Catholic like my mother, and a saleswoman for a country radio station. On the bathroom wall of her condo hung a photo of her with John Schneider, one of the stars of *The Dukes of Hazzard*. She was a short, round woman who knew a few jokes and whose dominant personality trait was extreme politeness. She never said anything compelling about herself and couldn't twist balloons into wild animals, but you couldn't help but like her.

She also seemed as unenthusiastic about homosexuality as I did. She never referred to my mother in a loving manner. They never made goo-goo eyes at the dinner table. For all anyone could tell, she was my mother's good pal. Maybe an old field hockey teammate from high school.

My mother wasn't very happy about this. To say my mother is affectionate is to say "Shakespeare wrote some stuff." My mother accosts perfect strangers with bear hugs. Not to be able to hold and kiss the woman she loved in her own home must have been pure torture. Out of respect for me, even the most innocent of romantic contacts — holding hands, a delicate touching of a knee, a reaffirming peck — stayed behind closed doors.

It must have taken some nerve for her to ask me. Maybe she thought I had finally come to terms. Maybe she was confusing me with someone else's kid.

"Hey, sport," she said. "I want to ask you something — and feel free to answer honestly. No pressure at all."

Uh-oh. When a woman asks you to answer honestly there are only two options: lie or fight.

"Yeah, what's up?"

"Well, Louise and I have been together for two years now. I was wondering — and, again, feel free to say no — if you would mind if we freely expressed ourselves around the house."

"What does that mean?" I asked warily.

"Well, do you mind if we . . . y'know, just touched each other like other couples do?"

"*WHAT?*" It was as if she had asked me if it was okay for them "to do each other in the public areas — y'know, really *screw.*"

"Oh, no no no . . ." she stammered. "Nothing obscene. We just want to be like normal couples. Maybe hold hands, hug, a small kiss here and there."

An overwhelming sense of power came over me, and I didn't like it. Although I wanted all gay activity to be restricted to, say, Mexico — I didn't want to have to tell my mother that straight to her face. At that moment, she granted me the authority to let her relationship naturally flourish among a healthy family environment. It was an opportunity for massive, life-changing growth. It might even decide the fate of their relationship.

"No, Mom," I said. "I'm sorry. I just don't feel comfortable with that."

The guilt blossomed immediately. I felt horrible. Oppressing someone is so much easier when you don't have to verbalize it, so much cleaner when executed through a series of silent maneuvers.

She immediately backtracked, trying to ease me out of my shame.

"Honey, that's completely fine. I respect that. Don't feel bad at all."

The power paradigm in our house shifted that day — for the worse. My trump card had been the threat of leaving her to live with Dad. That day she officially named me the love czar of our dysfunctional life together. If she wanted to have her son, she had to play by his rules. If ever I was spiritually aligned with Fred Phelps, Bill O'Reilly, and other moral fascists, it was then.

The divide between us grew. What had been a large chasm became the Grand Canyon of emotional disconnect. In order to act like a normal couple — to express her love for the woman she loved — she had to hide in her bedroom or leave the house entirely. Which meant our time together contracted even more.

The next day, Louise came over for dinner. She made small talk and told bad jokes. She was trying extra hard not to offend me. We ate a poorly cooked meal, and they disappeared. I watched gay-free TV in our gay-free living room — alone.

I imagined my mother, the night before, telling her, "No, sorry, I tried. He's just not ready to deal with it." They probably went to sleep wondering what life they were living where one of their own children not only disapproved of them — but had the power to banish them.

Chapter

17

You Might Be One, Too, Kid

ON A DAY WHEN HE WAS FEELING especially campy, God set in motion the world's longest practical joke: You will inherit your father's mammalian thicket of back hair. Your mother's ability to stay exactly ten years behind all fashion trends will pass unto you. That bulbous, alcoholic shnozz that has plagued every branch of your family tree shall bloom upon your face.

It's evolution's great balancing act. It's why actors now adopt pretty children from developing countries. They know that if they and their genetically superior spouses ever procreated, the children would come out looking like a cross between a Dallas Cowboy cheerleader and Benjamin Franklin.

My mother has many traits I would love to make my own. One of them is not being gay. I hoped that genetics would try to give me The Gayness and get it wrong —

accidentally giving me my mother's love of women. *Ah-HA! In your FACE, genetics!*

When I was eight years old, my father caught me holding up the *Playboy* centerfold of Susanne Somers next to the TV while *Three's Company* was airing. He laughed at my wide-eyed disbelief that the zany actress and the naked lady were the same person. And my choice in naked people was heading in the right direction.

Then, when I was sixteen, my mom did it.

She was standing at the edge of our TV room, in the exact same spot where she had asked if I minded if she and Louise casually embraced around the house. Apparently, the edge of our TV room was the Security Council of the United Nations of Gay Issues.

"Hey, sport," she said. "There's been something I've been wanting to talk to you about."

Oh god, what now?

"What's up?" I said.

"I just want you to know . . . I mean if you ever . . . even an inkling . . . think that you might be gay . . . you know that's okay, right? That it doesn't make you a bad person."

My face crumpled as if I'd just seen my teenage sister dancing naked to a classic rock song. "Why would you even SAY that?" I demanded. What the fuck *was* she saying? Was there a girlish prance to my gait? Did I not hold my posture erect enough or talk enough about sports and trucks?

And, oh Jesus, was she better at detecting it in others? Did it really take one to know one?

"I'm not saying you're gay," she said with a tender smile. "It's just important for me to let you know, that if you ever did wonder about the same sex, or had any feelings toward them, you have support. You're not alone."

"I am not gay. I can assure you of that." I glared. "And I'm pretty insulted that you're even suggesting I might be."

"Honey, no no no," she said. "Again, I'm not saying that you are. But, you know, people go through a lot of changes in their lives. In five years, you won't be the same person you are now. I didn't think I was gay at your age. But then as I matured, I got more in touch with my feelings and realized that that's part of who I am. I'm just saying anything's possible in life, and no matter what it is — I'm here for you."

"Do I *act* gay?" I snapped. At that point in my life, my sense of self-esteem could fit in a coin purse — with room left over for the coins. My self-identity was restricted to the fact that I knew my name and that I was born a male.

Had she and her lesbian friends been talking about my "gay potential"? If my mother didn't know she was gay when she was my age, is it possible that I was too immature to realize my gayness? Was homosexuality something that you didn't know you had — like an STD with a long incubation period? Would the gay portion of Troy one day send a message to the brain: *Look, the wrist and the groin and I have been meaning to talk to you for a while, and we feel you're old enough now to know the truth . . .*

"No, no, no," she said, for the fourth time. "But you will become a lot of great things in your life. You'll mature and evolve. And no matter what you think about gay people now — gay people *are great people*. When I was getting ready to come out of the closet, I didn't have anyone. No one stood by me. I want to make sure that if you ever feel anything like that, you won't go through what I did."

"Yeah, thanks for that," I snarled. "I can guarantee that will never happen. I'm pretty much the furthest thing from gay, Mom. Just because you are doesn't mean I have to be."

She tried to explain further — pleading the innocence and benevolence of her mission here at the Security Council of our living room as I foamed away.

I stormed into the bathroom. I stared angrily into the mirror. My reflection stared angrily back. I flexed a little. I turned my head from side to side. I tried to pace the bathroom floor to see if there was any prissiness to my walk, but the room was too small. *Gay?* I thought. *Fucking incredible. Fucking gay?! She has lost her fucking mind.*

That conversation added fuel to my suspicion that my mother was secretly, subtly putting me through some sort of gay training. First the doll, then the duffel bags with rainbows on the sides, then the after-school kids of gays group, now this. Maybe she was trying to raise her own support group or was simply trying to get a status report on her secret project?

A show of support is only valid if it's given for something for which you want or need support. Paranoia strangled me for months. This conversation coupled with my own fear of being gay by genetic proxy to form a super-complex of self-doubt. I started talking in a forced, low voice. I talked about girls incessantly, detailing the ways in which I had great, straight sex with them. I overcompensated with a vengeance. My friends must have thought I was an asshole.

Years later, I learned that — around the same time of this conversation — my mother asked my father if he thought I was queer. Even if my father thought I was a three-alarm flamer locked into a hellish, downward spiral of blow jobs and denial, he wouldn't admit it.

Neither would I.

The scariest situations are those in which we can see ourselves. If Americans see a television clip of a great white shark attack off the coast of South Africa, it's almost fascinating. "Quick, honey — you gotta see this! Holy crap — there goes a leg! Awesome!" — *smack!* — "Look!"

Consider, however, a South African surfer who frequents the beach where the attack took place. And let's say he's got a fresh wound that spontaneously gushes blood from time to time. Barring an evolutionary miracle of the *selachimorpha* super-order, a Kansas corn farmer cannot see himself in a situation where a great white would attack him. The South African surfer, however, sees every bit of himself in that situation and therefore feels the maximum amount of fear. This is why I'm glad my mother was a lesbian. Or rather, I'm glad that my dad wasn't gay.

I didn't just love my father or idolize him. I wanted to fuse with him physically. He was a six-foot-three, manly, towering statue of what I might one day become. I mimicked everything he did. During long tennis matches down at the city courts, he filled a tennis-ball can full of water and drank it in three massive gulps. I sat in the bleachers with my own tennis can of water. I waited until he drank, and I raced him, always ending up with half a can of water soaked around the collar of my T-shirt. I mimicked his forehand. I mimicked his laugh. I even shrugged my shoulders when admitting that I'd done something inanely stupid, just like him.

If one of Dad's tennis buddies had dropped by unannounced and said, "Troy, do you know what a homosexual is?" our relationship would have immediately taken a turn for the nonexistent. I would have stopped emulating him. I would have forced myself to undergo a homemade deprogramming system in which I rid myself of all his characteristics. I would have found a replacement role model of manhood. With no other adult men in the immediate vicinity, I would have ended up a freakish cross between Telly Savalas and Sylvester Stallone, saying nothing but snappy one-liners.

On meeting a cute girl at school: "Who loves ya, baby?"

On her walking away, to self: "Yo, Adrian!"

To the angered boyfriend of the girl, who was not named Adrian: "You're gonna eat lightnin', and you're gonna crap thunder!"

Yet no matter how hard I tried, one by one his traits would manifest themselves in me. Them's the rules. And that would have exploded my fear that one day I was destined to get it on with my doubles partner.

Although she denies it, I believe the fact that Mom was gay is one of the main reasons why my sister had such a hard time. Although Kim was fiercely independent from a young age, girls emulate their mothers. Even if their mothers play softball and hug like men. Kim could see more of herself in our mother, and it sufficiently scared the crap out of her.

In my case, well — thank God it wasn't Dad.

Chapter

18

My Great, Dwindling Humanity

THE GREAT THING ABOUT BEING a teenager is that there's no shortage of ammunition with which to kill your brain cells. According to the people who study such things, two cans of Coors beer will cure overpopulation of the hypothalamus. Smoke a joint and a village of brain cells commits hara-kiri before exiting through the nose in a snot rocket.

According to my father, alcohol and I had our first encounter when I was two years old. He had taken me to the county fair — the kind with genetically superior farm animals, carnival rides, and people who wash down deep-fried Twinkies with a smoke.

My father's not that kind of person. He was there to see a concert. But if there's one thing that bridges the gap between music fans and people who raise competitive pigs, it's beer. My father had all the ingredients for a good day — a picnic blanket, live music, his son, and a Budweiser. His contentment lasted until the third or fourth song, when a distressed matron tapped his shoulder.

"Do you know what your son just did?!" she scolded.

He looked down at me, and in my pudgy little hand were the few remaining ounces of his tall, cold one. I have always been a fast drinker. I probably breast-fed like a frat boy. Barring hard-partying midgets or lawn jockeys at the concert that day, I was the most plastered three-foot human in the vicinity. My father carried me away in shame.

By my senior year, alcohol had become my coolest friend. Drinking it in large quantities transformed me into a mythical, fearless creature who accomplished great things. Such as a capella karaoke, unprotected sex, and vomiting.

My mother was gone almost every other weekend, at physical therapy conferences or retreating to her lesbian place — which, as I had told her, could be out in the woods, in Cincinnati, wherever. Just not in my home.

Most weekend nights she was gone, and anywhere between 15 and 200 teenagers — and the occasional twenty-year-old boys who attended community college as a means of killing time between high school parties — experimented with ways to defile their bodies in our house. The first gathering was mellow — I invited four people.

"What are we gonna do?" a friend asked.

"Drink," I said.

"Oh, cool," he replied.

Later that night my friend and I lurked in the parking lot of our neighborhood grocery store.

"What about that guy?"

"No way, he looks like a cop."

"What about her?"

"She's got two kids with her, retard."

We figured the trick was to spot a male in his early twenties, someone with fresh memories of being tragically unhip. You needed someone who looked like he could benefit from feeling cooler than seventeen-year-olds begging strangers to buy them beer.

Then we saw him — a pale guy in glasses with prominent acne scars. He looked as if he'd lived his life on the wrong side of cruel jokes. The sort of guy who builds model jet fighters.

"Hey, bro . . . will you buy us some beer?"

"Huh? No, no," he stammered. "Can't do that, no way."

"C'mon, man, please? We've got girls waiting for us right now. You know what that's like."

"Of course I do. But that doesn't mean I'll buy you beer. You'll have to steal it from your parents like everybody else."

But by that time we were out of the car and had committed ourselves to it, so we just asked everyone. Eventually, we found a woman who appeared to be in her late thirties. She smelled like cigarette smoke and sour milk.

"How much you want?" she said, looking over her shoulder. She had the voice of a man.

"How much will twenty bucks get us?"

"A couple six-packs. What kind of beer you want?"

"The good kind."

"Just give me the money. I'll get you what I can. Which car is yours?"

We pointed to my lime-green Honda. The front

bumper had fallen off in a minor accident, and duct tape held the headlights in place.

"Go wait in it," she said.

Ten minutes later, she came out with two six-packs of beer and no change. We were pretty sure that beer didn't cost $10 a six-pack, but we didn't argue. She could pocket the extra money and spend it betting on cockfights in Mexico for all we cared.

Of course, those four friends I invited magically showed up as twelve. One of them had a half-empty bottle of whiskey. Another had a fifth of vodka minus a few tumblers' worth. The missing contents of a few parents' liquor cabinets gathered on my mother's dining room table.

We all sat around listening to Run DMC and drinking cocktails with grotesquely disproportionate alcohol-to-mixer ratios. We talked about which girls in school were sluts and which teachers we'd like to have sent to prison. We played strip poker until someone was actually on the verge of getting naked. Then we quit. No one got laid. For some reason, talking about which girls were sluts didn't increase our chances with the ones who were present.

By the end of the night, two guys I barely knew laid facedown on my living room floor, another on the couch moaning as if poisoned. A couple had taken my mother's bedroom, tainting her sanctuary with dry-humping. Six others — all of the remaining single girls — got into their cars and swerved on down the road.

After that, the parties improved. We mastered the art of getting people to buy us beer. We learned that disheveled people who looked like they took drugs were the best bets.

The twenty-two-year-old geeks proved blatantly uncooperative. We even got cocky, demanding our change from the malodorous alcoholics.

Then, bored, we started to "wahoo!" beer. "Wahoo!" is when you enter a liquor store, grab a twelve-pack of beer, and take it to the counter. The incredulous clerk, with a smug smirk on his face and arms folded, demands to see ID. That's when you grab your beer, yell "wahooooooooooo!" and run out the door.

Initially, we only did this at Pinocchio's — a nearby liquor store owned by an elderly Iranian man whose hunchback complemented his limp. He was also senile. So although we rotated who did the wahooing, we could eventually restart the rotation because he couldn't remember who had wahoo'd him in the past.

Eventually, the owner recruited his twenty-something son to stand guard. Each time we entered the store, he looked at us with daggers in his eyes. It was a look that said, *Go ahead, do it. I can't wait to snap your femur with my hands.*

His arrival forced us to find other liquor stores run by senior citizens. We had no scruples, but we had beer.

"Hey, Troy, this your party?" a group of sixteen-year-olds would say after self-consciously creeping up my mother's walkway.

"Sure is. I don't have a keg. I don't have a band. But everyone you want to party with is inside. Three bucks each."

"Really? C'mon."

"Yep, really. If you don't want to pay, that's fine — I've already got too many people."

I made anywhere between $100 and $500 a night and

only granted free admission to the Filipino wannabe gang members. It was a small bribe to ensure they didn't steal heirlooms or beat someone to a pulp to feel like real gang members. Eventually, I just hired them to work the door. They received a cut of the profits and a sense of entitlement. Instead of standing in a circle gawking at girls, they stood at the door and took money from the girls' boyfriends.

At this point, I was a proto alcoholic who occasionally smoked weed. But I never did hard drugs. My father had sufficiently scared the crap out of me with a graph that showed the peaks and valleys of drug use. "When you get to this point, you're just taking drugs to feel normal again," he said. "Over here, this is about where you die."

For most of 1990, seventeen-year-old girls danced to AC/DC on my mother's coffee table, torturing drunken teenage boys with partial stripteases. Cheerleaders went into my bathroom in groups to freshen their makeup and snort crystal meth. A quiet nerd of a girl gave oral sex to an upperclassman in my bedroom in front of twelve of his horniest friends, who energetically offered advice. Whatever parents prayed their teenage children didn't do when they left their sight, they did at my house.

But I had an ironclad strategy for these parties. I let them get to the critical moment where people are loose and high and thinking about having sex on the nearest flat surface. That's when I kicked everyone out. We sent a few handpicked girls into my mother's room. The cops showed up a half hour later and found a handful of aimless teenage boys in the living room watching TV.

"We've gotten a few noise complaints from your neighbors," they said, obviously unimpressed with the size of the "rager" a concerned housewife had reported. The house may have looked freshly burglarized, but it was not actively harboring excessive fun.

"Man, glad you're here," I said. "We called you guys, too. I invited a few friends over and word got out that I was throwing a party. I didn't know what to do for a while, but eventually we managed to kick 'em out."

"Do you have a keg?" they asked.

"A keg? No, not at all. I mean, we had a couple beers, but no keg. It was never even supposed to be a party."

They walked around the house, searching for drugs on the countertops that I had wiped clean just minutes before.

"What's in here?" they'd ask.

"That's my mom's room," I said, praying some plastered girl didn't giggle behind the door. "She locks it when she goes out."

Unimpressed, they issued their standard exit speech and left.

Partying wasn't the point. The point was obliterating structure. I was a catholic hedonist, truly feeling alive only when dangling one foot over the edge of my little life. Attending class became optional, depending on if it was a good day for surf. Or if anyone was willing to ditch with me and smoke cigarettes in a parking lot somewhere.

The day the high school dean called me into his office, I was sure I hadn't broken any rules in the last forty-eight hours. My mischief had boiled over into my academic career, my report cards dancing their way down the alphabet. You see, I had learned to forge my mother's signature perfectly.

I appeared at Mr. Kamon's doorway, and he was leaning back in his chair with his hands interlocked behind his head. He wore a self-satisfied smile — like a used car salesman who'd just sold a muscle truck to a grandma with glaucoma.

"Hey, hey, Mr. K. What's goin' on?" I said, falsifying pep.

"Mr. Johnson," he said, drawing out his syllables. I couldn't tell if he wanted to gossip about a new hottie transfer student he'd just admitted or if he knew he'd finally caught me.

"Don't be shy. . . . Come on in. Take a seat."

My mother was sitting off to the left. She held in her lap a huge stack of papers that I recognized instantly.

"I think you two have met," Mr. Kamon glowed. *Shit.* "Mr. Johnson, do you have any idea what your mother is holding?"

"Uh, not really," I lied.

"Those would be thirty-two notes excusing you from full days of school. Not one period, or a half-day here and there. *Entire days.* Do you have any idea how many days of school there have been *total* since the beginning of the school year?"

"A lot?" I said.

"A lot. Yes, you could say that. Sixty-two, to be exact."

"That sounds about right," I said, as though this would all clear up in a minute. If both of my lungs had collapsed and I had to eat nothing but liquid steak, I could still have attended school more than I had. I was convinced truancy officers drove their little vans, parked somewhere, and smoked pot — because I had never seen one.

"At first I thought you had some serious health issues," Mr. Kamon continued. "I thought maybe I'd have my wife cook some chicken soup for you. But now I'm beginning to think that no one would've been home if I showed up with soup, would they, Mr. Johnson? And that's not fair to Mrs. Kamon."

My mother was going to cover for me, surely. The sad fact was, I wore the pants in the family by the time I reached high school — and the shirt, and the shoes. The whole power ensemble.

It wasn't that my mother was born with a foam spine. She had survived Catholic school and had the scarred hands and psyche to prove it. She had raised two snotty kids largely by herself while earning a master's degree in physical therapy at one of the nation's top universities. She ran the spinal cord division at the largest veterans' hospital in San Diego and lived as a gay woman in the Reagan '80s without hanging herself. The woman was tough.

But her parents had both died before she was twenty-two. Her brother, a schizophrenic, lived in an apartment in Arizona, which he never left. Her sister was an alcoholic. When she was outed, friends stopped calling and strangers told her God didn't want her anymore.

So all she had left of a family was her growing peer group of lesbian friends, army vets with broken bodies, and me. A teenager blessed with a phantom heart, I used all of the above to get her to do my bidding.

"Troy," my mother said, smiling sheepishly, "I didn't write *any* of these notes."

"Of course you didn't," I agreed. "I did." I was going for the innocent-by-sheer-gall approach. It failed miserably. I was assigned to summer school that day, plus three months of Saturday school. By the time I was finally kicked out of high school for bringing beer to a dance, I knew my dean better than his children did.

Being told never to come back to Mount Carmel High School was the greatest thing to ever happen to my sex life. Although I had scaled the social totem pole as "the kid who throws the parties that never get busted by the cops," I was still second-class. I was marginally attractive, yet awkward and high-strung. I was on the tennis team, which to this day is fighting a long, involuntary battle with the chess club for the crown of lame.

At Poway High — a school ten minutes east — I was fresh meat. The girls had grown up with most of the boys in their classes. By the time they were ready to start experimenting with their clothes off, their most accessible partners were like siblings. And sibling sex was frowned upon in California — for now.

"Hey New Kid on the Block: will you go to prom with me?" the banner read. It was from one of the attractive blond twins who anchored the Poway swimming team. It was the worst decision of her senior year. Our prom together consisted of juvenile conversation mercifully interrupted by twelve cigarette breaks. She swatted away my hands until I threw up and passed out.

I continued to throw parties at my mother's house — now attended by kids from both my current and my former high schools. I slept with a different girl every few weeks, my need for sexual conquest outweighing any concern over my declining reputation. The nickname "Trashball" fit the bill.

My friends didn't help much, either. They, after all, were the kids who had organized The Great Car Rally. This genius idea involved making a list of delinquent behavior and assigning a point value to each. Ordering a Coke at McDonald's and then throwing its contents into the face of the cashier was worth 20 points. Stealing a golf cart was 100 points. Crapping on a cop car was 200 points.

They distributed the list around school. Out on a deserted road, sixty eager kids met and formed twelve carloads of teams. Each team received a judge who rode shotgun and tallied their points. That afternoon, these sixty kids terrorized suburbia. A McDonald's employee, his face dripping with orange soda, chased my group into the parking lot and bashed the doors of our pickup truck with a broomstick before we could speed away. Handfuls of teenagers streaked through the mall. A golf cart vanished and a cop car was crapped on.

The winning team got a half hour alone with a keg of beer before the other, less successful delinquents joined in. Later that night, the Poway police went on a manhunt, pulling over cars of teenagers to ask if they knew anything about a car rally.

"No, Officer," I told the one who pulled me over. "I'm just going to the movies with my girlfriend. What's a car rally?"

"I guess some kids really did some serious damage around town tonight — they're looking at jail time."

"Whoa," I said, worried that maybe a McDonald's worker had provided a police sketch artist with a remarkably true description of my plus-sized nose.

"Well, if you hear anything, let us know."

My days of hosting parties eventually ended. My execution and cleanup were usually flawless. I cleaned excessively, then dirtied the place in a wholesome manner — with clothes, tennis paraphernalia, and some food wrappers. An overly clean house would have raised suspicions.

But a half-empty can of Miller Lite — centrally located in my mother's underwear drawer — ruined my upstart career as a social coordinator. After that she asked my father to stop by every night she was gone. I knew this because one Friday night I opened my mother's front door with a full bottle of my mother's Beefeater gin in my hand. I was expecting to greet people who didn't really like me, but whom I called friends. And there was Dad.

"You're coming home with me," he said. Rather than obey his suggestion, I jumped into the Mercedes of the girl I was dating at the moment. Her rich parents didn't care if she snorted coke or harbored a runaway as long as she showed up for equestrian training. But after a few days, they suggested I leave.

I met my high school sweetheart — the love of my

young life — at the library, of all places. Jessica Windsor was a tall, slender, blond cheerleader with adorable, carefully placed freckles. She had a huge, beautiful mouth that shared a likeness with Julia Roberts and fresh lake bass.

"Who is *that*?" I asked my friends.

"That? Don't you worry about who she is. You don't stand a chance," said my friend Mark.

"Why?"

"She's a good girl. You, on the other hand, are Trashball."

Three months into our relationship, I was driving her back to her house on a Friday night. My knuckles glowed white with rage around the wheel.

"Troy, don't," she sobbed in the passenger seat. "Why are you doing this?"

"Are you going to sleep with me?"

"Why is it so important?"

"It just is. We've been dating for three months. THREE MONTHS!"

"I'm just not ready yet. I love you. *Please.*"

"That's not good enough."

I dropped her off and drove away as she sobbed on the sidewalk outside her house. Although my heart sunk when I looked in the rearview mirror and I actually cried on the ride home, I still considered repentance a form of weakness.

Incoherent Rage 1, Troy 0.

Jessica's parents rightfully hated me. I was a monster, emotionally disfigured. But I was infatuated with her, even thought I loved her. So the next night she accepted me back. Many people considered me ripe for second chances.

We dated for the remainder of the year, interrupted only by a short split because a ruthless, coldhearted girl with great breasts told friends she wanted to sleep with me. Dating me was also Jessica Windsor's worst decision senior year.

At the end of the year, I submitted my "Senior Thought" to the high school yearbook. It read: "To all the girls I've hurt — sorry. Nah, I'd do it again." A savvy and no doubt horrified high school editor thankfully omitted my entry from the book.

The night before our last day at school, friends and I camped in the canyon behind one of their houses. I drank whiskey from the bottle until I fell down in the dirt. A hard shake on the shoulder woke me up. A police officer was standing over me.

"C'mon, bud, get up," he said.

My blood alcohol level was still possibly lethal. I stood and tumbled backward into the smoldering ashes of the fire pit. Amid my friends' snickers, another officer said, "Someone take care of this one, okay?"

We arrived to our final day of school three periods late. My ceramics teacher handed me a note from the principal. I walked down the hall to his office, my blue pullover sweatshirt smeared with soot, looking homeless.

"Three Saturday schools left, Troy," he said. "How do you expect to graduate?"

"I dunno. I was hoping that begging for mercy might work."

He drew something on a piece of paper and pushed it across the desk.

"What's that?" he asked.

It looked like a tree, but that made no sense. I was still drunk and unable to interpret his doodle.

"It's a tree, Troy, a Christmas tree. Merry Christmas."

I graduated that weekend, walking in a procession with the other, more promising teenagers. I posed for photos and smiled and kissed Jessica Windsor, who later became a model and moved far away from me. In those photos, I look like an average kid, happy to be surrounded by family and friends on his day of achievement. Really, I was barely human, totally dead inside.

More than a few religious family friends told me later in life that they prayed for me that day. Luckily, Chico State University's admission policy was simple: Apply.

Chapter

19

Growth Through Expletives

"Fukkkin' faggguhht!"

The words roared out of my mouth, uneven, like food I had no interest in swallowing. Grandma Dorothy wasn't the only one, it seems. It was my first year at Chico State University, where a good portion of the student body minors in rehabilitation. I was drunk.

I had been waiting to scream those words since the day I found out my mother was a queer. A twelve-pack of cheap beer, a few shots of Jaegermeister, and a flamboyant gay man in a position of authority finally jarred them loose. And they nearly ended my college education.

Most middle-class American kids dream of going to college because it's like Willie Wonka's Vice Factory. Instead of a chocolate river, running through campus is a class-5 rapid of jungle juice — obscene amounts of alcohol mixed with obscenely sugary fruit juice — which leads either to

ugly people's first sexual experience or someone choking on their own vomit. Instead of lollipops and gelatinous candies hanging from the trees, there are marijuana joints handpicked by half-naked co-eds. Instead of Oompah-Loompahs, there is a hippie jam band that will eventually tour with Dave Matthews.

College is the first place where eighteen-year-olds get to live independently. They are free of their parents' tyrannical rule, but also immune to and sheltered from the laws that govern the rest of adult society. If an adult misses large amounts of work, he loses his job. If a college student misses large amounts of class, he gets to hang out with the marijuana-picking co-eds. If excessively truant, he will receive a letter from the university that reads, "You have been placed on academic probation. You will now be required to maintain a C-average, which we refer to as 'not doing well but not genuinely retarded.' Please join us on Sunday for an ice-cream mixer in the dormitory common area!"

Parents dream their kids will attend college for different reasons. They view higher education as the final stage of the life-preparation assembly line. Ideally, higher education prevents their offspring from working as telemarketers for diet-pill companies, giving birth to multiple children who run around like dirty-faced vermin in a double-wide mobile home. It also keeps their grown children from moving back home and shagging high school girls in the basement.

College does attract kids who want to do better for themselves. Some want to get into medical school and purchase a luxury automobile. Others want to convince the

U.S. government that cannabis is essential as a high-yield textile crop. Most simply want to become better human beings by reading a lot and discussing international labor laws at keg parties.

I arrived at Chico State with a few goals: to be emancipated from the shame of my gay mother, to party as though my liver were made of titanium, and to win a new car.

My father knew I was the *HMS Titanic: A Metaphorical Sequel*. I was a vessel of promise attracted to icebergs. And hurricanes. And seedy ports of call. This was his last chance to point to the huge, pretty slabs of ice approaching and say, "Might wanna put down that cocktail and turn this bitch around, son."

Wanting me to succeed and knowing that materialism was one of my dominant personality traits, he promised to buy me a car if I finished my freshman year with a GPA of 3.5 or higher.

I seemed destined to be the proud new owner of absolutely nothing — especially since eight of my close friends from Poway High School had also enrolled in Chico State. We all lived in the same dormitory and collaborated on its demise. The week before moving in, we had a few beers and took a vote. I won by a landslide. After a few months, the group decided, I'd be back in San Diego working at a chain restaurant and shagging high school girls in my father's garage.

The year was 1991. *Playboy* magazine had documented Chico State's reputation as a haven for intellectual miscarriage, ranking it the country's "Top Party School" in 1987. Nestled in a small agricultural oasis about 100 miles north of Sacramento in Northern California, 12,000 eighteen- to twenty-four-year-olds lived within four square miles of one another and terrorized the town. The college represented an inexpensive option for parents to send their kids who hadn't excelled in academics, but who also hadn't dropped out to become dope dealers.

Chico natives were, understandably, a nervous bunch. During summer breaks, they emerged, happy and carefree, shopping along the quaint downtown streets. They rode their bikes through Bidwell Park, where in 1938 Eroll Flynn did his gay forest-hero impression in *The Adventures of Robin Hood*. As students filtered back in each new semester, residents vanished. We reckoned they hid in bomb shelters, afraid frat boys would show up at their doors with plastic cups asking where the keg was and if they had weed.

My father accompanied me to orientation weekend. As part of his motivational strategy, he taped a blank piece of paper to the brick wall of my dorm room. "This is your future, Troy," he said. "Right now, your life is a blank piece of paper. A clean start. Now it's up to you — you can draw a beautiful painting, or you can fill it with graffiti."

I looked at the piece of paper and thought about what sort of life I would draw there. I knew I didn't want my life to be a pastel watercolor where heavily medicated, beautiful people relax in the gentle ocean breeze. I also didn't want to become Picasso's *Guernica*, with deformed semihumans dying all sorts of horrible deaths.

The next morning Dad picked me up for breakfast. Our dorm room smelled of stale cigarette smoke. At least sixteen crumpled cans of Keystone Light lay in the corner.

My roommate Ian and I looked as if we had found a hole in the space-time continuum and managed to age forty years overnight.

"All *riiiighhht* . . . looks like you guys had a party," Dad said, playing it cool.

"Yeah, getting to know the neighbors, y'know."

He looked up at the piece of paper.

"I see you've thought about your future," he said with a halfhearted chuckle. "Well, at least it's got nice boobs."

Every college dormitory has a resident advisor. These are twenty-somethings who get free housing in exchange for making sure you don't overdose on pot brownies or fail out due to a nasty Super Mario Brothers habit. The R.A. of our wing was Nick — an avian East Coaster whose face appeared to have been pressed in a vice until it jutted forward at a sharp angle. He chewed tobacco, was studying geology, and was fond of saying, "I'm getting my degree in rock, baby."

A soft-spoken girl with beauty-queen looks and a mind-blowing butt, Christy oversaw the girls' wing. Whenever she walked down the boys' hallway, freshmen heads popped out one by one like prairie dogs to have their minds blown.

Billy, a tall black man with pierced ears, ran the entire dorm. He looked and acted like Little Richard, wearing T-shirts with the word *Tolerance* below an image of two men kissing. He was the gayest man I had ever met — the lisp, the floppy wrists, and the gait of a prima ballerina. Nick and Christy attended gay rights rallies with him. The rest of us made jokes about the many uses of his anus.

Shortly into my first semester, my mother called with the news.

"Hey, hon, how's my big college man?"

"Good. I'm taking an African-American history class. I'm realizing what assholes we white people are."

"Yep, yep, yep." She laughed. "We've got quite a history to live down."

We chatted for a while. No matter what I thought about her being gay, I told her everything. If you can trust anyone with secrets, it's a woman who spent years keeping a big one from the family in her own home. Plus, what could she say if I drank too much or saw *Star Trek*'s Dr. Spock in the clouds after eating hallucinogenic mushrooms? Her alternative behavior obviated her from denouncing my alternative behavior.

"Look, now that you're at college," she said, "I've been talking with Louise about moving in to her place. But I wanted to talk to you about it first. To make sure you were comfortable with that."

"Of *course!*" I said, as if shocked that she would think otherwise. That new arrangement would give me a good excuse to live with Dad when I came home for breaks.

"Really? You wouldn't mind?"

"No, Mom . . . it's your life. Who am I to tell you what you can and can't do?"

"Great. Thanks so much, honey. That means a lot to me. I love you, turkey lurkey."

I was lying, of course. My gay mother merging with her gay lover to form a gay superpower fell just below "find herpes donor" on my wish list. But I was 600 miles away from all that now. Without her baggage, I could become a new person.

My first semester was a blur. Now that everyone *expected* me to fail — and my dad held out the carrot of a new car — I studied as if academic texts were the new cocaine. I entered the study hall every morning around 10 A.M. and didn't emerge until dinner. But every night, my friends and I grabbed our plastic cups and guzzled cheap keg beer until we fell over.

That first semester, our dorm room smelled of cigarettes, sex, and urine. Blacking out on a regular basis allowed me to develop a unique capacity to wet the bed. At least three times that semester, I woke up with a naked girl and a pool of pee beneath us both.

I was initially mortified. But with my grade-point average soaring, I took pride in my reputation as the "guy who gets straight A's during the day and parties like a rock star at night." I was the love child of Albert Einstein and Sid Vicious. I wasn't well rounded — more like a rhombus that emitted a bad odor. But it was good enough.

Every time the fire alarm went off in the dorm, the R.A.s were required by law to evacuate all residents to the lawn. This diversion provided a great opportunity to find out who was sleeping with whom. By the end of the year — as counted by the hall nerd — the alarm went off sixty-six times. The school newspaper wrote an in-depth story about the fire alarm epidemic at Shasta Hall. We set a school record.

"That fucking *bitch!*" screamed a freshman named Mike. It was 3 A.M., he was drunk. I was drunker. He had heard that a girl he'd been casually dating was canoodling with a guy from another dorm. He came out of his room with a towel around his fist.

"No, dude. Oh no," I begged.

"Fuck that!!! I wanna see the guy!"

He punched the tiny box of glass surrounding the fire alarm and pulled the lever. The piercing noise filled the halls. The alarm box shot forth a stream of greenish fluid, meant to identify whoever pulled it. It looked like alien urine. Mike glanced at me with wild, wobbly eyes, put his finger to his lips, and cackled like a crazy person. He ran into his room to hide the towel and within thirty seconds Nick the bird-faced R.A. was going door to door.

"Fire alarm! Which one of you fuckers pulled it? Everybody out! *Goddamnit!*"

The entire dorm shuffled out in T-shirts, pajamas, and boxer shorts — a half-drunk throng of freshman zombies, some with partial erections. Mike approached the girl he'd been dating, who was huddled under a blanket with the other guy. He called her a *slutwhorebitchcunt*. I pulled him back.

To curb our serial fire alarming, the R.A.s made us wait in the cold longer and longer each time it was pulled. This night, they were especially eager to prove their point. Someone had brought out a case of beer, and we were still drinking. An hour later, erections lost and the prospect of sex all but gone, the mob grew angry.

Students began shouting at the R.A.s inside, who were chatting idly. People in boxer shorts pounded on the glass doors. Christy opened the door and admonished the mob, "Look, you guys, you asked for this. If you don't want to wait outside in the cold, then tell whoever's pulling the alarm to stop."

Ian, normally an amiable, quiet guy, made a violent, jerking movement that suggested he was going to punch her. She recoiled. Gay Billy came to her rescue.

"Ian, that's enough! That is a threat of physical assault. We can have you kicked out of school for that!"

Ian chuckled drunkly and shuffled away. I took up his slack. Eight years of anger boiled up into a drunken rage.

"Fuck you, Billy, you fukkking fagguhhht! Faggggg-huuutt!"

The mob fell silent, a gallery of raised eyebrows and open mouths.

"He's a fukkking fag!" I protested.

A few of my high school friends snickered faintly, embarrassed for me.

Two days later, the school superintendent called me to her office.

"Sit down, Troy. Do you know why you're here?"

"Probably something to do with the other night," I muttered.

"We have some serious allegations about your behavior on, let's see . . ." She shuffled her papers to find the actual date. "November twelfth."

"I know. I was angry, I admit that. But the R.A.s had no right to keep us out in the cold for so long. People could get sick. They were just sitting in there, talking about . . . I dunno . . . Tom Cruise or something. Whatever they were talking about. They also yelled at my roommate without provocation."

Previous disciplinary encounters taught me that using big words relating to the law was an effective tactic.

"You mean Ian?" she asked.

"Yeah, he wasn't doing anything wrong, and they picked him out of the crowd."

"Actually, he made an aggressive threat of physical assault on one of our R.A.s. Four witnesses attested to that. He's been expelled from the dorms."

"What? That's not how it went down, but I doubt you'll believe me," I huffed, folding my arms. I thought about what I'd do with his vacated half of the room. I'd move his twin bed next to mine and make it into a king-size.

"Well, this isn't about him. It's about you using hate speech against our head R.A., Billy," the superintendent said, interrupting the mental blueprint of my new bachelor pad.

"Hate speech?" I replied, incredulously.

"According to four different R.A.s who were present, you called Billy — quote — 'a fucking faggot.' Troy, I don't know if you realize how serious that is. It's so close to a hate crime that we could turn this over to the police. Had anyone in that dorm assaulted Billy after your outburst, you might be in jail right now."

My stomach twisted. I imagined my father's face when I told him I was coming home to shag high school girls in his garage.

"You have two options," the superintendent continued. "Either you're expelled from the university, or you agree to undergo mandatory sensitivity training."

"Sensitivity training?" I stammered. "Oh, that's rich. Here's a little known secret about me — my mom's a lesbian.

If anyone knows gay, it's me. I definitely don't need someone telling me how to be sensitive around them."

"Well, I think Billy would disagree. And it's either
that, or you're out. You decide."

Two days later, Nick the R.A. called me into his
room. It smelled of tobacco juice and the thick cologne
musk I had decided was New Jersey's official state odor.

"Hey man, how you doin'? You okay?" he asked, genuinely concerned.

"I'm all right, man. This, though, is bullshit."

"Dude, you called Billy a fucking faggot. You don't see
anything wrong with that?"

"Billy's an asshole and sticks his gayness in everyone's
face. You don't see me wearing T-shirts that say, 'I fuck
women,'" I said. "I don't need sensitivity training. My fucking mother's gay. If you think I'm a homophobe, you've got
the wrong guy."

I didn't believe my own words. After all these years, I
had called someone what I'd always wanted to scream at
my mother — a goddamn fucking homo fag, a sick abom-
ination and stain on my life. I thought it would feel good.
Instead, as soon as it came out of my mouth I felt like I had
warts with long hairs streaming from them, zits and chan-
cre sores and pigmentation problems. I had exposed my true
character, and it was deformed.

In high school, I would have gotten high-fives for
calling Billy a fag. Someone would have told a joke about
two guys named Neil and Bob. In college — even at an ac-
credited keg party like Chico State — being a bigot was

worse than being on the tennis team. The shallow world-views you bring into college systematically self-destruct. In order to gain respect, you need to fight for the rights of gays, minorities, the disabled, the economically challenged, and various forest animals.

Nick escorted me to the public lounge. He popped a tape into the VCR. It was a movie about a gay kid about my age. People called him names and beat him until they eventually killed him. At first, I just did my best dead-eyed stare at the screen, trying to prove that I wasn't interested, nor needed, *this.*

"Well, I'll leave you alone, man. Just give it a chance," Nick said.

Halfway through, I cracked. In every scene where the goodhearted gay guy was belittled and beaten, I saw my mother. I thought of the friends who stopped calling her when she came out. I thought of telling my mother that I wouldn't allow any of that "gay stuff" in our home. I imagined some stain like myself calling her a "fucking faggot!"

I cried uncontrollably. I wished for an out-of-body experience, not wanting to be anywhere near myself. I had always liked to pretend I was okay with my mother's sexuality as long as it stayed out of sight. But I could feel the hate rising up in me. I could feel it fermenting.

Realizing you've been a total asshole most of your life is a tough pill to swallow. It's even tougher to realize that you've been a total asshole to your own mother. She had given birth to her own little cancer with feet.

I hit rock bottom that day, then crawled under that rock

and cowered. There were many reasons I was an alcohol suppository using sex as a substitute for self-esteem. There were reasons I was an emotional zombie concerned only with my own amusement. But of them all, it seemed hating my gay mother hit the top of the list.

I had to stop being who I had become.

Fuck, I thought, *this is gonna suck.*

Chapter

20

More Homo-Aversion Therapy with My Homeboy Jesus

THE NIGHT I HAD MY ASSHOLE SELF-REALIZATION, I prayed for the first time in years. I had come to view Jesus as Santa Claus with a conscience. With Santa, you just climbed onto his lap at the mall and rattled off the stuff you wanted: "I want a truck, and an Atari game system, and a new sister, and stuff that sets other stuff on fire. . . ." With Jesus, you had to barter for gifts. You had to offer up a few sins and promise not to cuss for a week or two. Only then could you ask for a replacement sibling.

I started small. I asked for forgiveness for my tirade against Billy. Strange, since I was pretty sure Jesus didn't like the gays. But I was also pretty sure he didn't go around calling them faggots when he was drunk. Then I asked Jesus to help me quit smoking.

That night my grandfather visited me in a dream. A heavy smoker who had died of cancer, he told me if I didn't quit smoking, I would die. Then a series of scary objects flew from the somnolent darkness — a skull and crossbones, a casket, a procession of zombies. It was like space debris of suck.

Finally, my grandfather's voice started rattling off statistics: *Eight out of ten people die if they keep smoking after age eighteen. Cancer will move from your lungs and infect your brain.* The voice kept getting louder and louder, eventually just repeating, *You will die. You will die. YOU WILL DIE!*

My arms flung out and struck something on the desk next to my bed. When I opened my eyes, I was hanging over the edge of the mattress facing the floor, sodden with sweat. The collectible Long Island Iced Tea glass was broken into five pieces. It was my favorite keepsake — tall and slender, with subtle silhouettes of nude women on the sides. My mother had given it to me in high school, and I had used it as an ashtray in college. Cigarette butts and a mound of ashes had scattered everywhere.

Ghosts are hallucinations. God doesn't make jaunts to state schools to work minor miracles on hungover freshmen. But the coincidence frightened me.

Frazzled, I got up to take a shower. I considered the plausibility of divine intervention. Was there a mathematical formula for it? Could it be figured out using a scientific calculator and the Pythagorean theorem? I thought about Billy, about straights and queers and alcoholics and cancer patients. Mostly, I thought about my mother. I'd spent the last seven years despising her — sometimes quietly, sometimes not so much.

I needed to change, but the sheer volume of my bad habits was overwhelming. How does an alcoholic smoker-bigot with a sex addiction transform into a nonsmoking gay rights activist who toasted chastity with a cup of decaf? Not easily, and not without help.

Lucky for me, amid the debauched intellectuals in a college dormitory, a few Jesus freaks always lurk. One of them was an acquaintance from high school — an unnaturally pleasant, rambunctious ex-football player named Trent. I went into his room that morning and asked him about Mr. Christ.

"So, Trent, what does being a Christian mean? Do you have any fun at all?"

"Yeah." He laughed. "Your version of fun may be different. I'm not going out getting plastered every night. But I don't think that's really anybody's true definition of fun, anyway. Seems a bit empty to me."

"Yeah, uh, I'm kinda getting that now. But, I mean, do you just spend every single day trying to be perfect?"

"Ah, heck no," he said. "No one's perfect. That's not what Christianity's about. It's just about trying to be a good person. If you fail, God always forgives."

"That's good — because I'm pretty fucking far from perfect."

"Did you ever go to church?"

"Yeah. I was raised Christian, but, y'know how it goes. Things changed. We stopped going."

"Sounds like you might be ready again."

"Yeah, I think I am."

"Well, no pressure, but if you want, I could help you ask Jesus back into your life."

And there it was. He read either from the New Testament or Holy Jim's Pocket Conversion Kit™. Broken, desperate, and in no way ready to come to terms with my gay mother or my faulty self, I became a born-again Christian. It was avoidance through prayer. For the next year of my life, I was the sort of person whom heathens cite as an example of why Christians should be exiled to an island far, far away.

I was a super-Christian. I stopped drinking entirely and attended church functions three to four days a week. While my friends went to keg parties, I attended "get togethers" with other twenty-something friends of Jesus, watching PG movies and sharing stories about "our walk with God."

A friend asked me how I was doing and I responded, "Well, I've just been working on my walk with God." As if this walk were a competitive one, in which Nike sponsored us. *Yeah, God and I failed to qualify last year, but I'm confident that with a stronger training routine we can crack the top ten.*

When I told my mother that I had become the most annoying Christian on the planet, she smiled. The sort of smile that polite people give when their gut is telling them to say, *That's a terrible, terrible idea. You should stop doing that immediately.*

When she came out, she snuck out the church's back door. She successfully pulled her children out, too. I'm sure when she sent me to college, she felt especially insulated from hard-core Christian condemnation of her lifestyle.

Those who become religious after freshman year usually convert to some Eastern religion that includes meditation, drum circles, and a little weed. That's because in college you take courses like "Magic, Witchcraft, and Religion," in which you study how whole nations of people believe that a butterfly impregnated a slab of driftwood and created mankind. And how others spend hours a day praying to an orblike "presence" that just started popping out the human race, like a chicken squeezing out a cosmic omelet.

It's hard to look at a thousand different takes on the same concept — how the hell we got here — and conclude, "All that don't jibe with what Mommy taught me must die." Unwilling to write everyone else off, it usually makes you conclude *everyone* is wrong. The people who think driftwood got knocked up are wrong. So are the ones who think people carjack because a naked woman in a garden ate some fruit. In the presence of higher education, solid religious beliefs usually crumble until you find yourself at a social gathering saying, "I believe in *something* larger than us — call it a god if you *must* — but let me tell you about the indigenous people in Africa who think that the North Star is the beautiful carcass of the world's first life-giving entity. . . ." Higher learning makes Hasidic Jews get haircuts.

Yet somehow, in the face of all of this education, I became a Jesus freak. It proved a certain imperviousness to logic on my part. Or, really, a wholesale rejection of it.

My born-againity naturally made my mother nervous. Even as a spiritually bankrupt party whore, I hadn't been especially thrilled about her gayness. Now I'd joined forces with a group of people who had a long history of lethal homo hating. But spirituality was important to my mother. Nuns had bloodied the backs of her hands as a kid. She raised us to be Christian. Even after coming out, she held a loose, unofficial belief in something larger than herself — so she cautiously welcomed my new path.

That path took me, along with a busload of Christian college students, to Palm Springs for spring break my freshman year. Palm Springs is a tiny oasis in the eastern California desert. For most of the year, its sole purpose on earth is to keep old people safely quarantined on golf courses. But it had a famous past as the place where stars like Elvis came to snort blow off locally made sandwiches. Milking its glamorous history, every spring break the city's small strip of nightclubs hosted America's intellectually exhausted, booze-parched collegiates.

My Christian friends and I came to save them. A former bed-wetting alcoholic myself, I played a key role in this saving. We stayed in the gymnasium of a Palm Springs Christian school, like a traveling basketball team. During the day, we walked along the strip and handed out Jesus pamphlets.

A hungover group of attractive twenty-year-old girls walked by, and I approached them. "Hey, how you girls doing?" I said.

"Fine," they grumbled, skeptical that maybe I was an

early starter, drunk by noon and trying to get them to perform wild sex acts in the nearest public bathroom.

I made small talk, asked them how their night was.
Then I said, "Yeah, I used to party a lot, too, but then I found
God. Best hangover cure ever. I don't want to be creepy
about it, but if you've got a minute, I could share with you."

As soon as I hit the word *God*, at least two of them
looked away. Sometimes, they just grabbed their friends and
walked off. But usually one very nice young girl — possibly
one who'd gone to church when she was younger —
humored me. She listened as I told some of my party stories, always ending with, "But Jesus is always there, when
the people you party with leave in the morning." She took
my pamphlet. She even passed the first dumpster without
dumping it.

We spent one night watching a Christian rock band
perform on the large patio of a club. The band actually
didn't suck — they had the mainstream potential of Pearl
Jam and a minimalist punk edge reminiscent of Fugazi.
Unsuspecting partyers stopped and got into the music.
Then they heard the singer lean into the microphone and
belt a chorus of *"His is the blood on the thorn / His is the
sweat on your brow / He's the Father, the Son, the Holy Ghost /
Get ready to bow."* That's when the realization hit people
mid-sip. Frat boys paused, looked at each other, laughed.
They immediately pounded their drinks and left.

But one girl took a liking to me that night. She was
a pretty brunette who'd drunk herself into supernatural in-
coherency. After hearing my God talk, she didn't walk away.

"Oh, I yousshheego uh shurch," she said. "Yehhr cute."

Very briefly, I considered taking her back to the gymnasium and having sex with her in several positions. I winced at the thought, then asked her to pray with me. That's when her friends came over and grabbed her.

"Leave her alone," her friend snarled as they pulled her away. "What, do you just wait around for some drunk girl like my friend here and then ambush her with your creepy religious talk?"

"No, no, no," I said. "We're just talking."

"Well, you're a creep. Just as bad as all the other guys here who try to take drunk girls home."

She was right. I couldn't even save with tact. I approached religion in the same manner as everything else in my life — with obsessive, excessive consumption. I returned from spring break nearly as creeped out by my religious self as I had been by my morally bankrupt former self.

However, for the first time in my life, I had truly believed I was responsible to someone besides myself. Jesus broke through my narcissism. Even as I annoyed my friends and lost a few, my liver returned to its natural color. I even stopped smoking for a year.

Jesus also helped me accept my gay mom. Ironic, I know. At the church I attended, the pastor refused to say whether homos were hell-bound. I asked him straight up: "So, whaddyou think — hell or no?" He simply said, "We're in no spot to make that call."

I didn't fully endorse Mom's lifestyle, but my time as Jesus Christ Superstar bound me by oath not to condemn her for it. The hate slipped away, even if for the time being it lay beneath a heavy coat of blind, creepy, religious love.

For my sophomore year, I moved into a house with Trent and another born-again Christian. We seemed primed to start our own religious commune that featured many Disney movie marathons and banging parties where people drank extraordinary amounts of soda. By the middle of the year, however, I had taken to smoking a little pot every night on our back porch. My Jeep appeared less frequently in Calvary Chapel's parking lot. My walk with Jesus came to an end, but my walk with Mom had taken its first few awkward steps.

By the time I was a sophomore in college, liberalism was starting to take hold. It happened to all of us. When we first arrived, two high school friends lived together in a dorm room with a window overlooking a giant, grassy quad where other students studied, laid around, and engaged in assorted tree-hugger activities like hacky sack and Frisbee. From that window they draped a Confederate flag. Occasionally, they even cranked up the volume and played Guns N' Roses' "One in a Million" — a song with the lines, *"Immigrants and faggots / They make no sense to me / They come to our country / And think they'll do as they please / Like start some mini Iran / Or spread some fucking disease / They talk so many goddamn ways / It's all Greek to me."*

None of us was surprised the day two black students knocked on their door for a tense discussion of the flag's purpose. Nick the R.A. questioned their choice of décor, and eventually all of us shamed them into taking it down.

Whatever prejudices you bring into college systematically self-destruct. If you hate Muslims, you'll end up in a study group with one and realize she's a better person than you are. If you're a hippie-bashing Republican, you'll end up dating one of the idiots who voted for Ralph Nader. If you're a misogynist, a feminist will change your life.

That is higher education's great contribution to mankind. It's not that universities crank out rocket scientists. It's not that creative writing courses serve as therapy for eighteen-year-olds who have daydreams about a gun, a fast-food joint, and a manifesto. Higher education creates an environment where a small mind is worse than a small penis. Not expressing empathy for race, religion, political affiliation, socioeconomic standing, and sexual orientation is like having a gastrointestinal disorder that causes you to explosively pass gas in solemn social situations. It's still okay to binge drink and take enough drugs to get a family of eight high, but one off-color joke sends you spiraling down the social totem pole.

Of course, it depends on your field of study. The knuckleheads majoring in geology still have some wiggle room for sexist banter, since women don't tend to study rocks. Business majors must retain some right-wing sensibility, simply because Fortune 500 companies don't take direction from migrant workers in Birkenstocks.

I entered the creative writing program, which harbors more alternative life-forms per capita than any other area of study. Walt Whitman presides as the patron saint of bookish queers. Charles Bukowski attracts anarchic punks like my friend Jesse, who had a bar code tattooed on his neck, accented by his fully shaved head.

Forced to interact with queers and punks and people with OCD, I actually started to learn about them. A young lesbian named Karen in my Introduction to British Literature course told the greatest jokes, mostly at her own expense. She became my first homo friend, poor girl. She had no idea how needy I would be. She was my portal into the gay world — the third-party case study through which I learned about my mother's people. And I was the annoying little kid who wanted to know why the homos' sky was blue and why their grass was green and why they had mullets.

Before one midterm, we found ourselves in an all-night coffee shop after the rest of our study group had decided that a little sleep was worth a B-minus. During a break, I seized the moment.

"Y'know, my mom's gay," I told her.

"Really? Wow, what was that like?"

"Oh, a bunch of hate and resentment and uncomfortable family dinners. When did you know that you were?"

"Pretty sure I was queer in kindergarten," she said.

"No shit?" I was shocked. I thought being gay was something you had to develop later in life, possibly because a member of the opposite sex made love like they were having a seizure, depleted your life savings, and disappeared with your cat.

"Yeah, I had a crush on Lucy Harris — blue eyes,

pigtails, super-cute dresses. I used to stare at her all day, every day. I used to be so excited for Show and Tell because I knew she'd get up and tell me something about herself."

My mother lurked in Karen's face. Maybe, in grade school, she ogled a girl in pigtails and a cute plaid skirt. Maybe she felt shamed. Maybe she promised God she'd never, ever do that again.

"Have you ever liked guys?" I said.

"Yeah, sure. I dated boys up until my senior year in high school, but it never felt right . . . just weird. The sex sucked — I wasn't into it."

"Was it hard for you to come out?"

"Hardest thing I've ever done in my life. Lost a few close friends. My father still treats it like I joined a cult. We have family get-togethers and he always asks me to 'try not to be so obvious.' It's been nearly two years and he still asks me if I've met any nice guys lately. But the hardest thing was dealing with it myself. I felt like a freak. I had to convince myself that I wasn't just a perv."

"I hate to ask this — and you can tell me it's none of my fucking business — but was there ever any . . . Did you ever have a bad sexual experience . . . I mean, any molestation at all?"

She laughed. Apparently she'd heard this one before.

"Ahh . . . the old 'Are you queer because a straight person fucked you over?' theory. No, not unless I've blocked it out. Don't get me wrong, I've dated some twisted lesbians who had been through some shit . . . but not many. I don't think you have to be broken to be queer."

Every culture has its assholes. I'm sure that high in the

"Oh, gosh . . . I think it was sometime about a year after your dad and I split. I just really fell for Tattle Dyke."

Boring, I thought.

"Did you lose friends? Is that why we stopped going to church?"

She answered mostly with simple yes or no answers. Being a gay person sounded pretty dull.

"What hardships have you encountered? What's the hardest thing about being gay?" I asked.

"Well, with me and Louise, it comes down to sex. She was raised very strictly Catholic and has some real problems with intimacy. She's got a lot of guilt about being a lesbian."

Eeeew, fucking gross. Sex wasn't supposed to enter the conversation. I wanted her to expound on the sociopolitical machine and layer upon layer of institutionalized bigotry that she'd hacked through with an emotional machete of resiliency. I wanted stories about storming the state capitol with a rainbow flag and choking through a cloud of tear gas to take on riot police. No such luck.

"Well, I'm sure I'll have more questions once I start getting into the book," I told her. Then I ate my Burger King Whopper, forcing it down as my throat quivered with a severe case of the heebie jeebies.

I didn't apologize for years of treating her like a freak. I didn't mention the hate or the resentment that I was terminating. But she knew. She smiled, rubbed my head, and ate her Whopper.

"I'll fully support you in the book," she said. "You just let me know what you need."

Chapter

21

Suspecting Your
Genes of Treason

IN 1993, MY SECOND YEAR OF COLLEGE, *Newsweek* ran a cover story that read, "Gay Gene?" *Newsweek* wasn't in my orbit. It was a boring magazine with too many stories about old white men and too few photos of Heather Locklear in a bathing suit. But this story got my attention.

It jumped out at me from the magazine rack at the liquor store I frequented daily for cigarettes, sodas, and over-the-counter amphetamines called Mini-Thins — tiny pills invented either by God or Timothy Leary. Or by God through Timothy Leary. These beautifully packaged pills helped me — and many others — atone for missing 60 percent of our classes. Pop a few and your eyes were physically unable to blink, let alone shut, for 72 hours. They've since been outlawed.

But what held my attention that day was the gay issue of *Newsweek*. There was no way I could buy it. First, the clerk, also the owner, slept somewhere in the back among the boxes of Doritos and stacks of kegs. If he missed a day of work, it was because he was observing a religious holiday, such as the Monster Truck Extravaganza coming to town. He knew damn well that I was in college for the chicks and the beer. I wasn't the sort who bought serious magazines as ancillary learning tools. He would suspect something.

I imagined what would happen the following day if I bought this "Gay Gene" issue. "One Coke, a pack of Marlboro Lights," he would say before glaring over his shoulders and leaning down to whisper, "You know, I'm not one to mess in a man's business, but the new issue of *Playguy* just arrived."

"What? You mean *PlayBOY*, right?" I'd stammer.

"Well, I saw you bought the gay issue of *Newsweek* yesterday. I see a lot of things. And if you're — you know, how do they say? — a sword fighter, then I understand *Playguy* is for your people."

I would be forced to march over to the magazine rack and buy *Playboy*, *Penthouse*, and a box of tampons — "for my *girlfriend.*"

Children of straight parents would never be so ridiculous. After all, it's *Newsweek*, not *Unzipped*, for chrissakes. But they also hadn't worried since age twelve that some rogue gay gene lurked in their genetic caste system, poised to kill off all the hetero genes with color-coordinated free radicals.

That *Newsweek* article was material evidence that

would no doubt surface in a plastic baggy at some sort of fraternity initiation.

"Before the elders vote tonight whether to bring Pledge Johnson into full brotherhood, we need to analyze the facts carefully. Sure, Johnson has shown great progress in his ability to swallow a cup of beer whole. But, gentlemen, it is my sworn duty to present to you exhibit A — the fag issue of *Newsweek*."

A whole room of boys with bad tattoos and burgeoning beer guts would raise their eyebrows and leer at me through the corners of their eyes. Someone would recount the time I refused to participate in a gang-bang with the chubby sorority girl who thought self-esteem was a type of manpowered vehicle. They'd cite how I was known to take poetry classes — and not just as a way to bed slutty goth girls. They'd try to think back to whether they had peed next to me in the john, and they would shudder. The nay votes would come swift and in large number. They would order me to leave, handing me my copy of *Newsweek* as if the pages were stuck together.

I tried to see if the gay-gene article was somewhere on the Internet. But at the time, the Internet was all hype. For all the claims that it would revolutionize the world, it took hours to upload a single page of text. And that page contained only a promise that the real, revolutionary page you were seeking could be found by uploading another page.

I'd have to interact with another human to get ahold of the story.

So I went to my dresser and pulled out my "I Am the Man from Nantucket . . ." T-shirt. My father had given it to me as the final, and most classy, in a series of phallic tees. The first batch included the entire line of "Big Johnson" shirts, in which white-trash men did funny things with their extraordinarily large penises.

I drove twenty minutes south of Chico to a town called Oroville. The fallow residents of Oroville thought the only good use for the business section of a newspaper was as toilet paper. They wouldn't know that "gay" was a synonym for their own term, "cock-sucking faggot." And "Gene"? Well, *sheeit* — he owns the rifle store and holds NRA meetings in his basement.

The first three liquor stores I tried stocked magazines like *Field & Stream* and *Barely Legal, the Slutty Cousin Edition*. I finally found a copy of *Newsweek* and padded it with some beef jerky and chewing tobacco.

Burning with anticipation, I pulled over a half mile down the road and parked my bright orange, 1979 CJ5 Jeep — which my father had bought me for getting straight A's my freshman year.

The *Newsweek* story reported the work of Dean Hamer. His research suggested that there may be a gene that caused a man to rub another man's rump while listening to Erasure. It included references to "linkage studies" and "variants" and other scientific crap. Bottom line: no matter how much hockey I watched or played, I might still end up a "bottom."

A knot immediately formed in my stomach — no doubt my gay gene bloating with confidence. The little fucker was doing a victory dance in my gut.

I had wondered about this for years. If my mother was

gay, was her womb a conduit for primordial homosexual goop? Would her appreciation for cat sweaters and team sports travel through the placenta, manifesting in me as a deep appreciation for antiques and real Corinthian leather?

The uncertainty tortured me. *Queer Eye for the Straight Guy* wasn't around in the late '80s and early '90s to make homosexuality cool. Being gay at that time was like being black in 1950s Alabama. You woke one night to the smell of smoke. You and your roommate scampered to the bay window of your Spindled Queen Anne home. There, on your well-manicured lawn, bearded men with clublike weapons were standing around a burning stack of Barbra Streisand records, glaring at you, *You're next*.

So I did what any normal, paranoid son of a gay person would do: I imagined having sex with men. If any part of me tingled or even the faintest of smiles crept across my lips, I would move to Madagascar and have my penis surgically removed.

I spent years bating my gay gene to show itself. Every time I did this, I nearly gagged. It was masochistic, but I had to know.

The suspicion of the gay gene had also led to epic promiscuity as a teen. This is not to brag about my nascent sexual prowess. Trust me, some of the women with whom I slept severely lacked both personality and dental enamel. Plus, you can overdose. Ask a hooker what she's doing on her day off, and the answer will invariably be boring everyday stuff like painting her carport or dusting her blinds. Whatever it is, it's definitely not fucking. Excess can strip the world's most pleasurable acts of their thrill.

My friend Doug was a virgin until age twenty. He's now thirty-two, and he still talks about casual sex as if he communicated with a unicorn and it told him the secret to eternal happiness. I sit there and pretend it's the same for me, when really my early sexual avarice has reduced the concept of a one-night stand from a mind-blowing experience to a "nice night I might share with friends if I don't forget."

I did have *some* standards — namely, that a girl's face not scare small children. But good looks, emotional compatibility, and living a life free of crab lice ranked far below how heterosexual having sex with a woman made me feel. I was protecting myself in case one day I discovered I did indeed have a gay gene. Habitually screwing women might establish a sort of irreversible pattern — the same way that my father can't eat any food besides peach oatmeal for breakfast. Gordon Ramsay could place a truffle-and-brie omelet in front of the man, and my father would longingly eye the box of Quaker Oats. If I established a similarly stringent routine, then not even Johnny Depp in silk Italian boxers would tickle my pickle.

Psychologists no doubt would have identified me as a sociopath and dedicated seminars to my teenage sex life. Around a flow chart of my sexual partners, they'd place thought bubbles that contained hearts and engagement rings. In my thought bubble, they would draw an image of me running from a gang of horny gays.

There was no personal growth for me during that time, no epiphany of self. I'm just lucky my penis never leapt from my body and ran shrieking door to door like a victim in a horror movie.

Chapter

22

You Can't Think Yourself
into Comfort

LOUISE HAS COOKED UP A JUICY FILET of steak and some spring vegetables. We're having cocktails — manhattans. I feel adult. Louise says something funny. My mother chortles and reaches beneath the table to touch Louise's knee — a loving, *I'm in love with your humor* sort of touch.

My body tenses. My smile strains. *This is good*, I think. *Yeah, good. Look at it. Play it over and over in your mind. Her touching her knee. Her loving her. Play it over and over until it seems like the most natural thing in the world. Like someone crossing a crosswalk, someone eating at a restaurant, someone watering a lawn.*

This is her life. This is her lesbian life. She is living with Louise now. This is what happens. There's no ceremony. There's no parade where a papier-mâché replica of my old, bigoted self burns in effigy and everyone drinks champagne until we're happy. We can only do this one uncomfortable moment at a time.

And so I make an effort to take part in her gay life. Not often — I'm not a terribly good son, as you may have noticed by now. But when my own overwhelming dramas and to-do lists and hours of wasted time cease to overwhelm me, I visit my gay mom.

In the beginning, I'm even proud of myself. I pat myself on the back for allowing my mother to be completely herself. Presented with the chance to know my real mother — not some pretend figure I've forged from the templates of a thousand straight mothers — and I feel like I'm doing a good deed. Like I'm a big person for this. *What a prick.*

No matter how much guilt I feel, no matter how much I want absolution by immersion, I can't have it. She catered to my shame when I was a kid, so I refuse to ask her to attend to my remorse. I can observe her life, I can support it, I can partake in it — but I can't own it. Her life cannot march in my own crusade against my past.

So the absolution I'm seeking slowly unfolds. It's not rapturous, instantaneous. There's no metamorphosis where suddenly I'm okay with everything gay. I've simply made a decision not to give in to the hatred and shame. But that still exists. I have to maim that part of me. It will never go away. My only hope is to diminish it, to make it so small that it cowers in the presence of my muscular, tattooed, black belt–certified sense of acceptance.

Chapter

23

Frat Boys Hate Fags, Too

AT A DINNER THAT INCLUDES WOMEN and at least one adult who finished high school, men can curb the desire to say, "The United Nations would be so much cooler if they wore gladiator outfits and decided nuclear policy in a cage match."

But assembled in a group of men, testosterone is dangerous. It leaps from host body to host body like a bundle of fierce, half-shaven electrons until it forms a tornado of electrified machismo in the middle of the group. The testosterone tornado spins wildly and emits deep-voiced, godlike sayings such as "I like tits!" and *"Yeah!"*

The prime environmental conditions for testosterone tornados occur in college fraternities — Roman orgies of machismo. Although technically considered men by government standards (they can vote, buy porn, and shoot foreigners), the eighteen- to twenty-three-year-olds who sign up to be frat boys are Peter Pans in search of one last Never-Never-Land.

I joined a fraternity my sophomore year. I blame the decision on free hot dogs, plus a deep-seated fear of living life cold and alone.

"Just come with me," said my friend Todd.

"No way, man. I don't pay for my friends," I replied.

"Dude, you don't have to commit to anything," he said. "Plus, they're giving out free hot dogs."

Free pork has always been pretty convincing. Living off a small allowance from my parents, I had taken to eating only very basic foodstuffs. The need for proper nutrition fell victim to my desire to pay for indulgent nights I regretted immediately.

Somewhere between my third and fourth free hot dog at the Delta Chi fraternity, I happened to run into a brother I knew from surfing in San Diego. He was a great guy — casual, easygoing, yet not socially catatonic — and he sported the most impressive white man's afro I'd ever seen. He introduced me to more guys who weren't the stereotypical frat boys with nice hair, good teeth, and the emotional maturity of a preteen.

If Jesus's stint in my life hadn't made my mother nervous, fraternity life was sure to scare the hell out of her. The fraternity's stance on homosexuality was simple: there are no homosexuals. Only fags.

Election into a fraternity paints a fascinating picture of social criticism. Each aspiring pledge is videotaped and asked to "tell a little bit about yourself." Most human beings

215

are not good at this. They stare at the camera, fidget, and reveal themselves to be the nerdiest, most undesirable life-forms on the planet. If the U.S. Citizenship and Immigration Services used a similar audition process, no new people would be allowed into the country.

At the end of rush week, all the brothers gather in the basement of the fraternity house. In an effort to curtail egregious heckling, alcohol is banned. And then the videos of prospective rushees are displayed.

Candidate 1: "Hi, uh, my name is Eric and —"

Unidentified Delta Chi brother 1: "Jesus! I thought the idea was to attract chicks!"

Candidate 2: "Hi, I would like very much to become a member of the Delta Chi fraternity because, from my observations, the solidarity is —"

Unidentified Delta Chi brother 2: "Nuhhhhhrrrrrrd!"

After twenty candidates or so, the brothers sneak outside and inhale alcohol. When they return, freshly inebriated, the activity gets even more interesting.

Candidate 21: "Hi, my name is Drew, and, oh, let's see —"

Unidentified Delta Chi brother 3: "Homo!"

At least three prospective brothers were laughed out of the running because, on videotape, it seemed as though they might snuggle stache-to-stache.

Frat boys' fear of the gays outstrips all others due to the very nature of "brotherhood." These excitably straight guys already engage in bonding and trust-building rituals that force them to swallow their fear of emotional vulnerability and man-on-man contact. A homophobic eighteen-year-old may feel sheepish about camping in the middle of nowhere with sixty of his closest male friends. ("Man, if we only had some chicks.") Add a homo to the mix, and the part where you're all drunk and aggressively hugging each other in a big circle may send him over the edge.

My entrance into the fraternity came at a particularly poor time. I was a freshly hatched liberal looking to understand gay culture. I also was taking creative writing courses, dialoguing daily with people who believed "sexuality is a fluid essence that is not a binary operation, but a life force that ebbs and flows, contained only by our desire to put it in a box and therefore squash it." Or something like that — put into iambic pentameter.

In a fraternity, frat boys dialogue daily about beer and pussy. These men find enormous pride in their ability to anchor a "boat race" — a relay in which two teams of six guys inhale 96 fluid ounces of beer in under thirty seconds. They scream, "Drink, motherfucker, *drink!*" until every drop disappears and they appear ready to vomit up a huge pile of Budweiser and dignity.

One night a few brothers came over to my apartment, a two-bedroom place I shared with another Delta Chi named Scott. We had bonded as the only ones in the fraternity with long hair who freely noodle-danced to hippie rock bands that played our socials.

Other than that, our living situation seemed pretty ripe for a double murder. I was a slob who smoked, adhered to a steady diet of burritos, studied midcentury poetry, and painted my toenails to get a reaction. Scott was a Republican who studied physiology, ran seven miles every night with his triathlete girlfriend, and burst into flaming fireballs of rage whenever four dishes piled up in the sink.

After a few beers, we found ourselves out on the balcony. Someone started a little game called Guess Which Delta Chis Are Homos.

"I'm telling you, Reggie is definitely flaming," said one brother.

"No, man. He's just shy," said another.

"I think we can all agree that Jamie is one hundred percent, grade-A fag," said another.

I started to seethe. Luckily, I wasn't alone. Also present was my friend Nate, a hippie liberal who found himself in the fraternity because his older brother was a brother. Nate and I spent many long nights talking about the meaning of life, using big textbook words and generic catchphrases from Eastern religions about which we knew nothing.

Nate also knew my mother was gay. During this Guess the Homo game, Nate cast me a sympathetic eye that said, *I know what you're thinking, but no.*

They went down the list of brothers. Between guesses, they told gay jokes.

"What did the two condoms say to each other when they walked past the gay bar?"

"What?"

"Let's get shitfaced!"

In my head, they weren't talking about straight guys, they were talking about my mother — my adorable, cat-sweater wearing, lovable, intelligent, beautiful mother. For the first time in my life, this wasn't okay. Tonight, what once had been a perfectly acceptable social exercise — homo jokes — stoked a rage in me.

But we were partying, and guys talk like this. We assert our manhood by jokingly destroying the manhood of others. *I should let it go. I should take a drag of my cigarette and finish my beer. Maybe go in and change the CD, maybe put on some Erasure and see if they get the joke.*

Like any new convert who's not well versed enough in his crusade to lecture the opposition, I did exactly that. "So, what would you do if you thought *you* were gay?" I blurted.

The brother who had been speaking looked at me as if I had asked what he'd do if he suddenly found himself in a crowd of ten-year-olds and had the urge to take his pants down.

"What?" He laughed, attempting to blow off the question.

"No, seriously," I said, "I don't think anyone in his right mind would *want* to be gay in America right now. That's like *wanting* to be a black man in 1950s Alabama. Doesn't seem like he'd choose to be beaten up and laughed at and creep people out unless he really, really felt like that was who he was. Don't you think?"

"Uh, you got something to tell us, Troy?" The brother laughed again. "I mean, that's just not being real. I would never find myself in that situation."

"I'm sure Jamie probably thought the same thing."

"Yeah, but that's his choice. I don't think he was born that way. Anyway, we're just havin' fun, man, c'mon."

"Either way," I replied, "if one day I developed the urge to give a guy a blow job, I would."

"*Whoa,*" said the brother, throwing up his hands. "Are you serious?"

"I'm totally serious. Think about it. How lame would you be if you really, truly knew that you were gay but didn't have the balls to act on it?"

"Well, you go ahead and do that, man," the brother said. "Let us know how it goes."

I didn't tell them my mother was gay. I didn't want them to think I was a crusader related to the enemy. I also didn't want pity to interrupt the breakthrough.

But there was no breakthrough. The balcony grew silent. They figured I was homo, or part homo, or just some flighty, impressionable liberal who painted his toenails to get a reaction. We drank in silence for a few minutes, made a few awkwardly mood-lightening jokes, and then everyone left.

Nate, who had stood silent throughout the whole interaction, gave me his take on the encounter. "I know what you were trying to say, man. And, in theory, you're right."

"But . . . ?"

"But this wasn't the time or the place."

"Those idiots were on my balcony, basically bashing friends — or so-called brothers — for being gay. And you know that's personal with me."

"Yeah, but sometimes it's too personal. You have to pick your battles, man. And trying to debate three typical guys after a whole bucket of beers wasn't the best place to declare war."

"Yeah, well, they're fucking retards."

"Maybe," Nate said. "But they're not the only retards you'll find yourself drinking with in your life."

He was right. I knew he was right. *Ta-da.* I had become one of the most annoying people on the planet — again. I was the college freshman who started volunteering at a chemical abuse center and, right when his friends were starting to peak on LSD, said, "Y'know, one tab of LSD destroys six million brain cells. You should see some of the patients I'm working with. The drooling's the worst."

I decided to plan out my battles strategically — maybe even keep Nate on retainer as a consultant. ("Okay, there's three dudes, one of them is from Oklahoma, the other is a Republican, but there's a liberal here who has a touch of a lisp — should I strike?")

Fraternity life was making less and less sense. There had been advantages — the sense of belonging, the "killer fuckin' parties!," the highly organized distribution system of promiscuity. But there was another reason I joined — the same reason I had hitched a ride on the Jesus train the year before: pure, unadulterated fear.

The concept of homosexuality had fractured my family. Thanks to the doll I got for Christmas and Gloria Fucking Steinem, I had feared that the mythical gay gene might be my heirloom. My mother had hinted that she thought I might be gay. And it didn't hit her until her thirties.

This gay thing seemed to strike at random. Learning to love homos increased the likelihood of it happening to me. The Big Gayness might sneak up on me while in line at the bank. I used these macho frat guys to form a heterosexual security blanket. If I ever found myself contemplating giving a guy a hand job for field research, I could stand next to Delta Chi brothers and howl man stuff over a foosball table.

But my self-esteem had finally outgrown its coin purse. After all the anger, the yelling, the loony bin, the dinosaur pump — I realized the Great Homo Threat was a lie.

I had discovered new threats — the fraternity brothers on my porch, Anita Bryant and Pat Robertson, and my own relatives. People who made the world a little bit shittier place for my mother to live because she loved a woman.

That night on the porch became the point of no return. I no longer felt sheepish about loving a homo. I no longer felt uncomfortable about sticking up for her in public. I felt compelled to do so. I dropped out of the fraternity within a year. I made this decision during a boat race in which men called each other motherfuckers with beer dripping from their well-crafted facial hair.

My epic run as a homophobe had come to an end.

Chapter

24

My Sister's Wedding

WE'D ALL SEEN THIS COMING. My sister announced she was getting married. Her fiancé, a peppy soccer player from the University of Las Vegas, blushed when he said, "Holy cow."

Early in life, my sister had set her mental periscope on the perfect family. She wanted the dog, the picket fence, and the Bible studies. If a breakthrough in obstetrics was made, she would have paid a premium for the 2.2 kids.

When most people plan a wedding, they organize a pretty exhaustive to-do list. Have it at a church with a man of the cloth presiding, or in a public park by a friend ordained by the almighty Internet? Offer a vegetarian meal or make the freaks eat cow? Invite all ancillary relatives who don't even know if you're still alive, or keep it small and intimate?

Very few add "Make sure Mom looks like a woman" to that list — but my sister did.

My mother maintains that her love of pantsuits started before she came out. It's true — in early pictures, our mother looks like the lead singer of The Monkees with breasts. But after the outing, her fashion sense dissolved from femininely androgynous to Levi's and cat sweaters. Her hairstyle oscillated between a bowl cut and a mullet. She hadn't worn makeup since her own marriage to my father. My mother was, and is, butch.

Sometime after calling my mother to break the good news, Kim called her again to inform her of the dress code — which had been designed specifically for her. Pantsuits were banned from the proceedings in no uncertain terms. My sister also made an appointment for my mother to visit the beauty salon the day of the wedding.

Sending my mother into a beauty salon is like sending an Aborigine into a computer store. She was nervous, disoriented, and painfully aware that everyone in the entire salon knew she had no business being there, that a daughter had sent her butch mom in for an emergency makeover.

"Did Kim tell you?" Mom asked me over the phone before the wedding.

"That she's getting married?"

"No, silly . . . are you ready for this? I'm going to wear a dress."

"Holy shit. Do you *own* a dress? I mean, one that isn't from the sixties?"

"Kim's going to take me shopping." She laughed. "I don't think she trusts me. She told me she needs to approve of my selection."

"Oh God. Don't tell me she's gonna make you wear heels."

"Yep. Although I told her they can't be too high, or I'll break my ankle. And get this."

"What?"

"I'm going to wear *makeup*! I haven't put on lipstick — God, twenty years, probably."

"You're gonna have to wear a name tag," I said. "A big one that says, 'Hello, my name is Kim's undercover lesbian mother.'"

"Well, y'know, Kenny's family is really religious. She doesn't want them to be taken aback. I understand that. I don't want any attention on the fact that I'm gay during her wedding."

We nervously laughed together.

On the biggest day of my sister's life — a day when she proclaimed her eternal devotion to one man, with whom she would carry on our family line — the lesbian wasn't invited. My mother could only come in costume. Imagine asking your ugliest friend to wear a veil to a club so she doesn't scare off hot guys. It was mean, tragic, and completely understandable. After all, just a few years earlier I had banished Lesbian Mom from public appearances *and* from the privacy of her own home.

On the day of the wedding, a hand touched my shoulder. I turned to see my mother smiling sheepishly as she held out her arms. Her look was a cross between *ta-da!* and *oh my God*. She was wearing a pink dress. A shade of deep, lusty red coated her thin lips and eye shadow sparkled above her eyes. No stylist on earth could have made that mullet feminine.

To others, she was a forty-something woman doing her best to look pretty on her daughter's big day. To us who knew, it was an unnatural transformation. She looked like a sophisticated transvestite.

"These heels are effing *killing* me," she said under her breath.

"You look great," I said.

During the reception, my mother sat at a table among other women in dresses. On the other side of the room sat Louise, her lover of eight years, who smiled politely at the other adults at her table, most of whom were seated beside their husbands, their boyfriends, or their dates. Louise looked awkward and alone. No matter how nicely you dress a lesbian, put two of them together and their cover is blown. My sister had intentionally separated them.

Chapter

25

The Afterlife

MY FATHER AND STEPMOTHER THREW a huge party when I finally graduated from college. Every relative and family friend came and a DJ spun. Before the party, my father called to ask how many bottles of liquor my friends would want ("Enough to get drunk and take their pants down"), what sort of music ("If I hear Kenny G, I'll re-enroll"), and which friends I wanted to invite ("The ones who will get drunk and take their pants down").

"Dad, this is awesome, I really appreciate it," I told him. "Y'know, it's gonna be a huge day for me. I'd like the whole family there. I'd love to invite Mom and Louise if you're cool with that."

I knew my father would be rather uncool with that. This was my chance — nay, duty — to help my father break the chains of bigotry. He was having no part of it.

"I have to tell you, Troy, I just don't feel comfortable

with that. I don't know what it is. I'm not racist, but I have to admit I'm a bit homophobic."

My mother didn't come to my graduation party.

Life continues to go like this. I continue to chase down my past. I continue to kick myself. It's a series of vignettes in which I get to know my mother for the first time all over again.

Some mistakes are irreversible. If you steal a stereo from someone's home and find Jesus on the freeway, you can always break back into the house and reinstall the thing. Maybe even install surround sound.

But when it comes to trespassing human emotions, you can't untrespass them. Every time I join my mother's gay life, it aggregates on top of all those bad memories she has of me as bigot child. It's like icing on a cow patty.

It will never leave me, the tiny little bigot in my gut. Sure, he's smaller, emaciated, begging for some TLC. *"Just one fag joke, please? It's just a joke. Lighten up. Throw me a bone here!"* But too much good has come of this change of heart. My mother has inspired me. If she can live through what she lived through, so can I.

Louise is family. I hug her like another parent. When I turn thirty, their separation after sixteen years together surprises me. With such a small share of the romance market — 10 percent, they say — I had thought lesbians held on tight until the ride was over. Gay couples, it turns out, are just like straight ones — loving, emotional, kind, inconsiderate, emotionally detached, and suckers for a pretty girl in a nice dress.

I sit in the living room of a lesbian couple in Oregon

who are my mother's friends. One talks about seeing my aura and how it shines. Her wide smile suggests heavy medication. She's endearing and creepy at the same time. Her lover raises sheep. Whenever they slaughter one, there's a ritual. They say a prayer for the sheep and the land and hold it in their arms as they slit its throat and cry.

I attend church service with my gay mother. I ask for details when she tells me she's got a crush on a woman who looks like the mother on *Eight Is Enough*, with the telltale short hair and a matronly femininity.

I go to a dinner party with six of my mother's butchest friends, two of whom have learned to belch the word *dyke* to the amusement of the others. This, too, unsettles me. The tension rises up in me until, finally, I burp "Straightguy" to the amusement of all.

I write for the *Gay & Lesbian Times* in San Diego. I do it because I'm a writer and am desperate for people who will pay me to write. I also do it because, in a small way, it supports her. I write about lesbian comics, I interview gay actors, I attend gay plays. Cross-dressing for a story called "Trans-Journalism" barely contributes to the gay community, but even if the drag queens who dress me up think of me as their little straight novelty toy, that's a good thing. It's only right that I jester for their amusement.

My (soon to be ex) wife and I head down to the beach for a meeting of the Silver Beaver Club — my mother and her middle-aged lesbian friends who hang out around a campfire, eat pasta salad, and laugh. A few of them test me, pushing my boundaries by talking about vibrators and telling racy lesbian jokes. I laugh and tell my own jokes. I'm not totally convincing — it's not completely comfortable — but I do it, and each time my laugh becomes a touch more genuine.

I worry about my mother. She lives in Talent, Oregon. A few minutes down the road one way is Ashland — a liberal hot spot known for college kids, Shakespearean festivals, hippies, and gay people. A few minutes the other way is Medford — a chaw-spit and gun-rack city that uses gay people as hood ornaments.

My mother is not an incognito queer. Her hair, tie-dye T-shirts, and sweat pants give her away at sight — to say nothing of the rainbow bumper stickers. I worry about drunk men chasing her off the road into the woods. Luckily, she's a lesbian and can handle herself. If my father were gay, I would smother him with chloroform and move him to San Francisco in the dark of night.

My gay mother has also immensely affected me — and my sex life. Women I date cannot wear flannel. They cannot look like they bench-press more than me. They cannot belch. They cannot cuss excessively. They may watch professional sports, but they must cheer daintily. They cannot exhibit any masculine traits whatsoever. Well, they can do all of this, but I can't date them. Chalk it up to that simmering gay fear.

My father and I even joke about it.

"Yeah, she's just not very soft or tender — she's not very womanlike," I'll tell him about yet another girlfriend.

"Yeah, you've got an issue with that. Well, you wouldn't be the first Johnson male to marry a lesbian, *ha ha ha.*"

The laws of physical attraction strongly resist intellectual reason. Some women — great women who drastically lowered their standards the moment we kissed — didn't realize what they were dealing with. They failed to be perfectly feminine, and I had to leave.

My sister still has issues, too. Over the years, she has drifted away from fundamentalism into a kindler, gentler approach to Christianity. Because of this, or simply because time is making good on its cliché and healing wounds, she and my mother have become closer — to the point that I often envy their relationship.

Kim's three children, however, had no idea that Grandma was a scissor sister until I gave my sister a copy of the manuscript of this book. At which point she told them.

To this day, Kim estimates that she has told five or six people our family secret. During their sixteen years together, my mother was always allowed to bring Louise to Las Vegas to visit my sister and the grandchildren, but they were never allowed to sleep in the same room.

"I still feel uncomfortable even saying the word 'lesbian' in public," my sister admits. "Isn't that ridiculous?"

Of course it's ridiculous. When we practice ridiculous for so long, we stop noticing it.

Chapter

26

It Never Ends

A BEAUTY QUEEN IS BEING DRIVEN SLOWLY down the street in a convertible sports car. She perches on the edge of the backseat, wearing a tiara and waving a dainty, professional wave. Her makeup looks three, four inches thick. You can hardly tell she's a man.

Behind her marches a group of volunteers, all in embarrassingly new T-shirts emblazoned with their nonprofit's logo. They hold signs that read "Healthcare for EVERY-ONE" and "Gay People Get Sick, Too."

For their entire sixteen years together, my mother and Louise had separate health care plans. Insurance companies must love gay couples. There's more money to be made in the homo market.

Then a busful of big, hairy men passes. They stick their round beardy faces out the windows, smiling to the crowd. Some of them are on a platform on top of the bus dancing. It's an old song — disco, possibly. Sasquatchian men dancing together to Diana Ross. Their features say *lumberjack*, their personalities say *princess.*

They are "bears." I learned this at last year's Gay Pride parade. This year, my girlfriend has come with me. Volunteers have festooned us with rainbow ribbons. Along the sides of the streets stand lesbian women, straight women, old people, young people, whole gangs of children. There are women who are manlier than me, with their 1950s greaser look — white T-shirt, sleeves rolled, arm tattoos, tight jeans, Doc Martens boots. They hold their pretty girlfriends around the waist and wave at the beauty queen.

I especially love this about homos — particularly about gay men. They, more than anyone except extremely young children and possibly black people, possess an enhanced capacity for fun. They don't stand around worrying how a certain dance move will affect their social standing. They don't consider excessive laughter a sign of a feeble mind. They infect you with their will to live.

Apparently, when you come out of the closet your social inhibitions stay in. Or maybe when the world treats you like an outsider, the only way to maintain a modicum of sanity is to embrace your outsider status fully. Judging by the world's stiff, polite, inhibited, reserved, shamefully dull existence, unbridled good times will assure your outsider status. Someone might even call the cops.

Some gays think drag queens and techno music and hairy men in leather do more harm for the gay cause than good. While lesbian politicians are trying to get the American government to view gays as a respected, valuable part of society, a silly little bear is doing the sprinkler atop a party bus in front of thousands.

But just look at them! Even this gang of dykes on bikes, their arms spread to the handlebars, the leather jackets, their bandanas, jeans, boots — they're smiling uncontrollably, giddy to watch people clap and whistle because they're dykes on bikes.

My mother doesn't ride a motorcycle. She drives a Honda — more sensible, better gas mileage. But she could ride a bike, maybe with one of those helmets with a metal spike on top. The crowd would whistle at her, too.

My girlfriend and I keep walking down the parade route. Last year, someone threw cans of tear gas at the parade. Lesbians and straight women and whole gangs of kids coughed and covered their mouths and ran away until the gas dissipated. Then the parade resumed.

This year, there is no sign of tear gassers. But what does a person who gasses a gay parade look like?

The music is awful. I've always hated techno. This is how I know I will never truly be able to be a gay man. I can't appreciate the *oom*-ching-*oom*-ching-*oom*-ching. Although, because I like to dance like a white man in public and embarrass the ones I love, I start to do what I think is the Running Man.

"Oh God, please stop," says my girlfriend, smiling nervously as she looks around to see who's watching. "Do you *always* have to be the main attraction?"

"Oh, you love it, you love it, feel it, feel it, move it, shake it," I say in rhythm with my dancing — which has no rhythm.

We resume walking. I feel a sense of connection with my mother, although I'm not sure she's ever attended a gay pride parade in her life. For me, it's the celebration I never got. No one baked me a cake or gave me a goodie bag with techno music when I snuffed out the hatred. This is my party as much as theirs — I too get to dance very badly and wear rainbow ribbons and wave to the drag queens. It announces my transition, the undoing of an American bigot.

And then we see the police. Six of them are sitting on big, beautiful brown horses. They are wearing helmets, sun-glasses, and — yes — moustaches. They're all so cop.

"You are a perversion of God's will! You are an abom-ination in the eyes of the Lord!" The man has a mega-phone. He is standing behind the beautiful horses. The cops are serving as a shield.

"Yeah, you, extend your middle finger — that's all you are! Degraded and hateful and perverted. God looks down on this event and all that it stands for. There will come a day when you will be judged, and you will spend eternity rotting in hell! Look at you — lost, perverted, de-filing what God has created you to be. You are the work of the devil. You are doing the devil's work."

One of the cops gives me an exhausted, empty smile. My girlfriend tugs on my arm to go.

"I wanna hang for a second," I tell her.

"We don't want to listen to these assholes," she says.

But I do. I am fascinated, reviled, energized. I recognize them. "I wanna hang out here for a few minutes. Why don't you walk on, and I'll catch up."

The look on her face says that she's not happy that I want to be here — that I want to leave her alone and listen to these people — but I can't leave. She doesn't need to hear this, but I do.

"Don't stoop to their level," she says, the old cliché. "Don't do anything stupid." She casts me a frustrated look and walks off.

The sidewalk here is completely bare. There are no lesbians watching, no straight people watching, no gangs of children within earshot. A gaggle of young gay males dressed in go-go dancing outfits prances by.

"Your life is empty, godless! All you have is the flesh and your wicked ways! You will burn in hell!"

One sprightly go-go dancer blows the protesters a kiss. Two others behind him flip off the protesters, smiling.

The main man with the megaphone has brought a stepladder. Perched precariously on the top step, his head peaks over the asses of the beautiful horses. He waves a Bible. Twelve or so of his people surround him holding picket signs that read:

"YOU WILL BE JUDGED"

"FORNICATING AGAINST GOD"

These are the people whom good Christians despise. They see me laughing.

"Go ahead, laugh! We'll see who laughs last! Scorn the

mountains of Tibet there's at least one small, bald man in an orange robe whom the other monks think is a real twat. But the only two queers I knew personally — my mother and Karen — were great publicists for the gays. Like Magic Johnson did for AIDS, they helped dispel the accusations, rumors, and the myths. They didn't bash straights for being sexually puckered. They didn't tell jokes about Mexicans and fences. They didn't even call anti-gay Christians *ratsonsabitches*. They knew what it was like to be treated like a herpes sore on the collective mouth of America.

Thanks to Billy, Karen, and higher education, the realization was sinking in. My resentment of my mother hadn't even been my own. Unable or unwilling to think for myself, cultural paranoia flowed through me. People of the cloth like Pat Robertson said gays were perverts headed for hell, and I had nodded. Politicians said they were seventh-class citizens, and I hadn't argued. Family members treated my mother like a leper, and I quarantined her in her room.

I needed to make reparations. For years, I had refused to know my real mother, or at least only agreed to know the parts that pleased me. It was time to put away my toy parent. She was coming to visit the following week. This would be a perfect time to admit my faults.

The rumors fly when a parent is coming to visit. An excitement hangs in the air. Unless you're from a severely poor family, parents represent touring philanthropy. They show up and take stock of their offspring's life.

A fridge sparsely stocked with ketchup and beer? *Check.*

Two Mexican blankets impersonating a comforter? *Check*.

An old issue of *Sports Illustrated* being used as toilet paper? *Check*.

Then they take you shopping. From eighteen to twenty, most humans have never been excited about the prospect of a twelve-pack of toilet paper. That changes when you're using a slick photo of Michael Jordan to wipe. Still, college students refuse to waste money on the banal necessities of life, so their apartments are full of expensive drugs and imported chocolate stout — but no toothpaste.

Even before she arrived, my mother told me to "think of what you need for your apartment, and we'll go shopping." When we took a breather from our spree at the local mall, I decided to come clean about how I'd been a total asshole and wanted to be involved in her life in every way possible.

"Hey, so I'm thinking I'm going to write a book," I said.

"Oh yeah, what kind of book?" she asked.

"About growing up with a gay parent," I replied, holding my breath and waiting to hear her say, "Try it, and I'll sue your ass."

"*Ha!* That's a great project — people need to know about it. And, well, you know about it. Need my help?"

"Well, yeah," I replied. "We'll have to do a series of interviews. I'll have to know everything about what it's like being gay."

"Well, I can tell you as much as I know . . ."

"Like, when did you first know?"

love of God! What he has given he will take away! You will gnash your teeth and wallow in pain!"

In Oregon, my mother is playing with her two dogs, throwing them a tennis ball, letting them lick her face. Or maybe she's down at the school, where she tutors kids who can't keep up. She is receiving her award as the best gay person in Oregon. She is living in peace.

"Queers!"

It's surreal, a farce. But then —

They are in my mother's living room. They are yelling at her through the megaphone. The dogs are barking. My mother tries to stay strong, stoic. They call her a pervert, an abomination, a person who goes to hell. *Don't cry, Mom. They're bastards. They've lost their minds.* A single tear appears, and then my mother starts to sob.

I am fifteen years old. I am in my mother's living room with the megaphone. I am yelling how much I hate her. What she's done to me. How she's shamed me.

The farce has ended.

I could dart past the cops, start swinging. I will hit the man with the megaphone first. I will bruise him with the New Testament. Then I will take on the others for hating my mother, for being embarrassed of her, for using the word fag in her presence, for standing at the end of the hall and yelling at her, for banishing her from her own home.

The cops are still sitting on their beautiful horses. A

mound of hot shit falls in front of the man with the mega-phone. I exhale a smile.

I turn to the parade again. The music is bad, but they're so proud, so electric. They keep blowing kisses. My mother is in Oregon playing with the dogs, happy. We are living our lives. There is so much more to do. There is so much more.

I am picking my battles. I am blowing them a kiss.